THE
WELFARE STATE
IN
CRISIS

By the same author:

*Society and Social Policy: Theories and
Practice of Welfare*

THE
WELFARE STATE
IN
CRISIS

SOCIAL THOUGHT AND SOCIAL CHANGE

RAMESH MISHRA

School of Social Work, McMaster University,
Ontario, Canada

St. Martin's Press   New York

Printed in Great Britain
First published in the United States of America in 1984

ISBN 0-312-86158-3

Library of Congress Cataloging in Publication Data

Mishra, Ramesh.
  The welfare state in crisis.

  1. Welfare state.   2. Social change.   3. Social
policy.   4. Economic policy.   5. Public welfare.
I. Title
HN65.M52   1984   361.6′5   83-40178
ISBN 0-312-86158-3

To the memory of
Tara Devi and Sushila D.

Contents

Acknowledgements

Thanks are due to Dr David Boswell and his colleagues at The Open University for many helpful comments on an earlier draft of this book, to Diane Allen and her team at the School of Social Work for secretarial support, to Cris Santos for compiling the bibliography, to Priscilla Harding for preparing the index and to Elizabeth Nagy for typing the final version of this book. The errors and shortcomings remain my responsibility.

Ramesh Mishra,
School of Social Work,
McMaster University

Definitions and Abbreviations

Differentiated Welfare State (DWS)
A welfare state in which the social welfare sector is seen, by and large, as distinctive and unrelated to the economic, industrial and public sectors. Also referred to as the pluralist welfare state.

Integrated Welfare State (IWS)
A welfare state in which the social welfare sector is seen as closely related to the economic, industrial and public sectors. Also referred to as the corporatist welfare state.

NHS
The National Health Service, or the socialised system of medical care in Britain.

welfare state
A liberal state which assumes responsibility for the well-being of its citizens through a range of interventions in the market economy, e.g. full employment policies and social welfare services. The term includes both the idea of state responsibility for welfare as well as the institutions and practices through which the idea is given effect.

Welfare State
Used infrequently as a shorthand for the post-war social system of the West comprising a mixed economy, a liberal polity and a social welfare sector.

Introduction

In varying degrees and forms, the welfare state throughout the industrialised West is in disarray. The outward signs of trouble are of course all too familiar. First, the onset of 'stagflation' and the end of economic growth – not only has the resource base for social expenditure ceased to grow but, more ominously, the welfare state is being seen as a barrier to economic recovery. Second, the end of full employment and the beginning of large-scale unemployment in some countries. Third, the 'fiscal crisis' of the state: partly as a result of the economic recession, governments in many countries face a yawning gap between the resources necessary to finance public expenditure and the revenue actually raised. While the recession has reduced government revenue it has added to public expenditure, e.g. through the higher costs of unemployment benefits. Fourth, a decline in the resources available to the social services followed, recently, by a deliberate policy of cutback in services in a number of countries. Fifth, a general loss of confidence in the social system of the Welfare State. The state's ability to manage the mixed economy, of which the social welfare sector is an integral part, is in serious doubt. In many ways it is this loss of confidence that is at the heart of the crisis. The techniques of state intervention in the market economy developed in the post-war years – conveniently labelled as Keynesianism – seem to work no longer. Indeed Keynesian forms of intervention in the economy increasingly appear as a part of the problem rather than the solution. More generally, the effectiveness of state action and therefore also its scope is in question. In short, both the practice and the rationale of the welfare state is in jeopardy.

This is an entirely new situation since the inception of the post-war welfare state. For, despite differences among political parties and sharp polemics among social scientists and others on the question of social welfare, the success of the welfare state used to be widely recognised. Grudgingly or otherwise, it was acknowledged as a system that had successfully combined private enterprise and economic growth with social protection and political stability. Few people thought seriously in terms of an alternative path of development for the West. This is no longer the case. The legitimacy of the welfare state is in serious doubt.

It is this problem of legitimacy, especially in respect of the social welfare activity of the state, that forms the subject-matter of this book. In short, it is concerned with ideological (or if it is preferred 'ideational') rather than political or economic aspects of the current crisis of welfare capitalism. This is not to suggest that economic and political issues are unimportant. That would be patently absurd. Nor is it to suggest that the ideological debate over welfare can be conducted meaningfully in isolation of economic and political arguments. It is rather to emphasise two things. First, that we are concerned with the broad intellectual responses to the travails of welfare capitalism rather than with detailed economic, political or philosophical (value) arguments. Even less are we concerned with identifying political groupings likely to support particular ideologies of welfare. Second, we are not concerned with the specifics of the economic or political problems facing western countries and even less so with the problems of any particular country. That said, it is fair to point out that much of our discussion is based on British and North American literature on welfare.

The book is planned as follows: Chapter 1 looks at the nature of the legitimacy of the post-war welfare state and the process of its erosion. Chapters 2-5 examine some major ideological orientations, namely the various diagnoses offered and the solutions proposed with respect to the crisis in welfare. Finally, Chapter 6 presents a personal view of the future of the welfare state in the light of the discussion in the preceding chapters, and argues that a 'corporatist' form of the welfare state could be the way ahead.

1 The Lost Legitimacy

The High Tide of Legitimacy

The affluent society and the consensus on welfare
It would be an exaggeration to say that the post-war welfare state enjoyed something like a universal consensus until recently. Since its very inception it has had its share of critics. Thus a small group of economists of anti-collectivist persuasion, of whom Hayek and Friedman are probably the best known, attacked the mixed economy and state welfare provision vigorously. The welfare state, they warned, was the road to 'serfdom' and economic ruin.[1] This viewpoint was also espoused energetically by a number of conservative politicians in most western countries. Yet what is distinctive about the 1950s and 1960s is that outside a small circle of faithfuls this anti-collectivism was never taken very seriously. Such ideas made little headway politically and even less intellectually. This is more true of Britain and Western Europe generally than of the United States, where the welfare state has never enjoyed comparable legitimacy. In principle, as a matter of political ideology, Social Democratic and Conservative parties differed sharply on social questions – one favouring collective provision of basic services the other market provision and voluntarism. But, in practice, both more or less hugged the middle ground (known in Britain as 'Butskellism') In any case, rhetoric apart, no practical politician could seriously advocate a policy of dismantling the welfare state and returning such basic services as health, education and pensions to market and voluntary auspices. State commitment to maintaining full employment, providing a range of basic services for all citizens, and preventing or relieving poverty seemed so integral to post-war society as to be almost irreversible.

But this is not to say that the welfare state had it all its own

1

way: far from it. Polemics against the welfare state were never in short supply. In Britain, for example, the rationale of the welfare state began to be questioned as the 'affluent society' took shape in the 1950s. By the middle of the decade full employment and steady economic growth began to look like a permanent blessing enjoyed by post-war capitalism. And by the late 1950s arguments against the welfare state became more insistent. The affluent society, it was claimed, had made the Beveridgian welfare state redundant. The entire paraphernalia of compulsory social insurance, as well as state programmes of health, education and housing, belonged to another age. They were devised for an age of austerity, privation, unemployment and the absence of economic growth. With full employment and rising personal incomes there was no need for the standardised, universal social provision envisioned by Beveridge for a war-ravaged Britain. The welfare state, argued the Right, ought to be rejected and replaced by increasing freedom of choice through private provision in education, health care and pensions. The wasteful and unnecessary 'universality' of indiscriminate state provision should be replaced by selective provision for the genuinely needy and poor.[2]

In the early 1950s, a plethora of evidence accumulated in Britain and other industrialised western countries to show that poverty had virtually been abolished, income distribution (even pre-tax) had become markedly more equal and on the whole a great deal of levelling, economic as well as social, had already taken place. It was widely believed that a variety of social changes, including progressive taxation and the provision of 'free' services to the mass of the population had taken the levelling process quite far.[3] Such findings provided a favourable climate for a counter-attack from the Right. Despite right-wing rhetoric, however, the broad consensus over maintaining the Beveridgian welfare state, ensuring minimum levels of living through a range of social services made available on the basis of citizenship, was never seriously in question. For if the anti-collectivists pointed to the fact of rising income and general prosperity, the collectivists began to demonstrate that increasing affluence did not mean that it was shared by everyone. Thanks largely to the work of a group of academics and social investigators oriented towards social relevance and concern rather than value-free social science, for example, Titmuss and Townsend in Britain, and Kolko and Harrington in the United States, post-war society showed itself to be a good deal less benign and egalitarian.[4] Whereas Galbraith writing in the mid-1950s saw poverty largely as a residual and marginal phenomenon, Harrington shocked America by demonstrating that something like one in five Americans, after one of the most prosperous decades in the country's history, was living in poverty.[5] More generally, social research in the early 1960s showed that in the rich societies of the West relative poverty was persistent if not increasing. In different ways, Titmuss in Britain and Kolko in the United States demonstrated that contrary to what had almost become conventional wisdom income distribution had not become more equal. Moreover official statistics, which formed the basis of the studies showing increasing equality of income, presented a picture that took little account of the reality of tax loopholes, fringe benefits, expense accounts and a host of other tax avoidance techniques which skewed 'real' income in favour of the upper and middle classes.[6] Social research in Britain, the USA and elsewhere began to reveal that in respect of poverty as well as inequality the promise of the welfare state was a long way from being fulfilled.[7] The conclusion was obvious. Far from being dismantled, the social services needed extending and reforming. Market forces, notably in their inegalitarian effects, needed a great deal of correction through state intervention and social provision.

If the decade following the war showed a seesawing of ideas around market and state welfare, the early 1960s saw the weight of argument shift in favour of the welfare state. It is against such a background that North America (both the United States and Canada) moved further towards developing state welfare provision.[8] The paradox of 'poverty in the midst of plenty', together with the political pressures generated through the civil rights protest and urban race riots, made it clear that a steady, annual increase in the GNP was not by itself going to solve social problems. By 1965 Wilensky noted that haltingly, carping and dragging its feet all the way, the USA too was moving towards some form of the welfare state.[9] Clearly if the USA, the Mecca of free enterprise and market capitalism, and the leader of the western world, was ready to embrace the notion of state responsibility for the nation's welfare, then the prospects for anti-collectivism were gloomy. True, the War on Poverty and the movement towards the Great Society were initiated by the Democratic administration (Kennedy and Johnson). But the landslide victory of Johnson against the right-wing Republican Goldwater in 1964 showed the strength of the liberal consensus.

Generalising across the western countries as a whole it could be said, without exaggeration, that in the 1960s, the correction of social imbalance through social programmes and services became almost a bipartisan policy. Radical attacks of the time on the politics of consensus, the 'administered' society and the 'welfare – warfare' state (social welfare at home and imperialism abroad) underline this point quite clearly.[10] Be that as it may, the point is that nowhere in the West was there an outright repudiation of state commitment to welfare. Social programmes and high levels of social expenditure were not confined to social democratic states. West Germany, for example, was ruled by the conservative Christian Democrats throughout its post-war 'economic miracle'. But far from repudiating the welfare state, Germany fashioned one of its most impressive post-war social programmes – a dynamic state pension scheme (1957) – in the middle of national economic resurgence under a Christian Democratic Chancellor.[11]

The point is that economic prosperity was a double-edged sword. On the one hand it provided the rationale for a reduction in the government's role in welfare and the privatisation of services. On the other hand, it could also support the argument that a society that was growing richer year by year could afford generous social programmes. Rising national income could augment both social expenditure and private incomes. Distribution need not be a zero-sum game; private affluence and public generosity could go hand in hand. In any case, social expenditure involved horizontal rather than vertical redistribution of resources. The welfare state was no Robin Hood robbing the rich to help the poor.[12] Moreover, far from being detrimental to the economy in any obvious way many social services – education being the prime example – were in fact meant to help economic growth directly.

Here, then, was a social arrangement with apparently few costs and many benefits which included maintaining social stability and fostering a sense of national community and solidarity. Not surprisingly, the consensus over social policy was widespread. A distinguished sociological commentator on welfare and social policy in Britain noted,

Less is heard in the middle sixties of the more extreme views expressed in the middle fifties – such as that social insurance should be abolished and replaced by a limited system of social assistance, that freedom should be given to 'opt out' of the NHS, or that people should be given 'vouchers' with which to buy places in private schools instead of being offered free places in public ones.[13]

There was, according to Marshall, a 'growing measure of agreement on fundamentals ... There is little difference of opinion as to the services that must be provided, and it is generally agreed that, whoever provides them, the overall responsibility of the welfare of citizens must remain with the State.[14] The issues at stake in the 1960s, wrote Marshall, were 'less concerned with social ideology' and more 'with social engineering'.[15] In a certain sense this was even truer of the United States, where technocratic conceptions of social management were held far more strongly. But in important ways American commitment to welfare remained half-hearted. 'Social engineering' meant something different in the American context. It had less to do with fashioning a welfare system that would provide a range of basic services to all citizens (as in Western Europe), and more with helping individuals and groups to function more effectively within a liberal market society. Without mimimising the importance of institutional change in American welfare – Medicare, for example – we could say that the major thrust of American effort in the 1960s was towards eradicating the 'culture of poverty' rather than poverty as such. In this sense, the War on Poverty and the Great Society programmes can be seen as forms of social work, even if conceived on a grand scale.[16] However, even if not all western industrial nations were fully committed to the welfare state ideal, it looked as if it was only a matter of time before they fell in line with the others.

It is not easy to generalise for western countries as a whole;

5

there are important differences in the scope of social programmes and the timing of their development, but, on the
whole, the period from the mid to the late 1960s represents the
high watermark of the welfare state idea. Western Europe had
already embraced social welfare; now North America was
about to do the same. Overall, the blend of affluence and welfare
appeared as a triumphant vindication of the western social
system. And social welfare looked like an eminently successful
way of tempering freedom with security, enterprise with
stability, economic growth with a measure of social concern and
amelioration. No wonder all western industrial societies seemed
to be moving, willy-nilly, in the same direction. Who but the
diehard ideologue (of the Right or Left) could doubt that the
welfare state was at once the correct and righteous path for the
West?

How was such an abiding consensus possible? We have, of
course, touched on some of the reasons for it already. But in
order to answer the question adequately we must look at the
sources of legitimacy of welfare in some detail. These explor-
ations would also highlight some of the basic assumptions
behind the idea of the welfare state – assumptions that are
under critical fire at the moment.

Capitalism made safe: Keynes and Beveridge
The post-war welfare state rested on two pillars – one Keynesian and the other Beveridgian. These, I should add, are
convenient symbols of certain new departures in economic and
social thought, and, of course, practice. Reduced to bare
essentials, the Keynesian element stood for the government's
ability to manage demand in a market economy through
judicious intervention, for example, by increased public
spending during a recession, especially with the aim of
maintaining full employment. The Great Depression had
shown that left to itself the capitalist market economy could
not function properly. The economic and social costs of
laisser-faire – in a drastic fall in production, mass unemployment, political and social unrest – were extremely high. This
waste and inefficiency of a market economy could be corrected
through moderate forms of intervention.[17] Keynesianism, in
other words, stood for state intervention from the demand side

6

of the economy to ensure a high level of economic activity and full employment. We might call this the 'economic' component of the welfare state. The Beveridge notion of insurance (in the wider sense) against the hazards of a market economy, on the other hand, formed the 'social' component. Unlike the Keynesian economic argument, the social argument for state welfare was, of course, not new. Since the days of Bismarck in Germany and Lloyd George in Britain, most capitalist countries had developed forms of social protection underwritten by the state. What was new, especially in the context of the English-speaking world, was that the principle of state intervention was made explicit, and the institutional framework which would make state responsibility for maintaining minimum standards of life a reality sketched in detail. This involved pooling society's resources and spreading the risks. Social insurance, understood in a broad sense, summed up this new departure. Universality of population coverage, comprehensiveness of risks covered, adequacy of benefits and the citizenship notion of the social services (provided as of right to all and not as a form of charity to the few) were the hallmarks of this approach.[18] Adding Keynes and Beveridge together we can see that the scope of state activity in western societies increased a good deal and also received a clear rationale.

Now both Keynes and Beveridge assumed that these forms of state intervention and service provision would *complement* the market economy. The overall intent was to make the liberal market society more productive, stable and harmonious. Implicit in this was the notion of a once and for all piece of social engineering, albeit on a somewhat large scale, that would correct certain structural imbalances stemming from economic and social *laisser-faire*. The entire operation was conceived of in terms of a positively functional relationship between the state on the one hand and the market economy and the social structure more generally on the other. Neither of these reformers saw any conflict of values or functions arising from the changes they were proposing. The intellectual and pragmatic rationale on which they had built the case for the welfare state left little room for doubt. Moreover, the wartime experience, at any rate in Britain, provided the basis for a powerful social consensus behind the proposed reconstruction. Indeed, more generally, the 'demonstration effect' of the war in respect of state intervention, especially in the wake of the disastrous *laisser-faire* of the 1930s, made the proposed reforms look quite 'practical' and non-controversial. As regards the functional relationship between welfare and capitalism, the modest collectivism implied in the Keynes-Beveridge approach suggested little room for dysfunctions or incompatibilities. The overall rationale of the reforms was that the relationships involved were positive and beneficial. Neither the market economy nor the class structure were to change in any radical way. It was a genuine reformation of liberal capitalism.[19]

It must be remembered that both Keynes and Beveridge were primarily concerned with solving the problems which had beset Britain and other capitalist countries in the 1930s. They could not have anticipated various negative consequences and limitations of the welfare state that would become more evident in years to come. True, Keynes for example was not unaware of the possibility of wage-push inflation in conditions of full employment. But such eventualities looked somewhat remote against the background of the 1930s. Moreover, Keynes felt that as an economist it was not within his brief to consider what was essentially a political problem.[20] In short, it was precisely this important problem of the 'political economy' of the welfare state that its architects failed to address. As 'reluctant' collectivists they had recommended a modest form of collectivism.[21] They did not foresee that the combination of a pressure group polity, full employment and comprehensive social welfare provision could give rise to various unanticipated consequences which would undermine the 'mix' of public and private activity represented by their design. That however is retrospective wisdom.

In talking of Beveridge and Keynes I have been thinking primarily of Britain. But in other western countries, too, especially in Europe, post-war developments were based on the assumption of harmony between the social welfare sector and the market economy. The post-war welfare state was above all a means of social and system integration. State action was a corrective, and state institutions a complement, to the market economy. Moreover, social legitimisation of a market society was an important function of the welfare state. Universal and comprehensive social programmes, such as income maintenance, health, education, personal welfare, expressed the idea of 'one nation' or 'national community' in conditions of market capitalism and class inequality.[22] In short, the welfare state was to make liberal capitalism more productive economically and more just socially. The proof of the pudding was in the eating. Post-war welfare capitalism was so successful, both economically and socially, that the success redounded fully in favour of the integrative assumptions underlying Keynesian and Beveridgian prescriptions. It would be a long while before the pudding would go stale and put the validity of these assumptions into question.

Social theories and the welfare state: the integrative bias
In functionalism, the dominant social theory of the two post-war decades, Parsons and others elaborated a theory of society which emphasised the harmonious and positively functional relationship between the 'parts' of a society.[23] Society was seen in terms of harmony, with social consensus at the level of values and beliefs and functional 'fit' or integration at the level of institutions. Social conflict, strain, tension and disequilibrium, were temporary phenomena more or less 'automatically' corrected through appropriate reactions from within society. This was, roughly speaking, the basis of the doctrine that social institutions 'evolved' out of functional necessity. State welfare institutions came under this category. Their main 'function' was to integrate – to co-ordinate and harmonise various institutions and groups within advanced industrial society in order that the social system worked smoothly. This ('logic of industrialisation') view of social change and the criticism levelled against it are too well known to need elaboration.[24] The main point to be made here is that such theories provided the rationalisation for the idea of development, once and for all, of a stable and harmonious advanced industrial society.

Functionalism and its empirical counterpart, the theory of modern industrial society, introduced two related notions which were influential in shaping our thinking about post-war western societies. First, the idea that social change (or more accurately societal change) has to be understood in terms of a

9

number of stages – in the first stage the social system is in stable equilibrium; in the second, forces of change destabilise the system, and new patterns, institutions and practices begin to emerge. These are not adjusted to one another and there is a great deal of strain, tension, anomie, and the like as a result. In the third and final stage new integrative institutions begin to develop and gradually restore society to equilibrium. Thus a simple model of stability (old society), change and disruption, stability (new society) was put forward and post-war society was seen as having arrived at the third or final stage.[25] The essence of this approach, as noted already, is that stability, harmony and order are seen as the normal state of affairs. Conflict, dysfunction, and disequilibrium therefore appear as problems of 'transition' from one type of system to another. This way of looking at social change invested welfare capitalism of the post-war years with a spurious stability and finality.

Closely linked with the above approach was the idea of a modern industrial society. What was seen developing worldwide was neither capitalism nor socialism – these were but means to the same end, different routes leading to the same destination – but the industrial society.[26] Market society and state-directed socialism, class struggle and the classless society, pluralism and totalitarianism – these dichotomies were also a product of the transition. The advanced industrial society transcended these antinomies. Among other things, this meant that the economy of western societies was seen as 'industrial' rather than capitalist. In the context of the disastrous economic dislocations of capitalism in the inter-war years this was an important shift in perspective. The focus of attention moved away from the economic relationships of a market system to industrial technology. An industrial economy, according to this theory, required substantial state direction. A large state presence, including welfare functions and services, was seen as necessary for the effective functioning of an industrial society.[27] The thesis of 'convergence' included social welfare, and researchers tried to show that irrespective of political and ideological differences state welfare programmes were developing in all industrial societies.[28] More generally, the state was seen as the integrative agency *par excellence* of advanced industrial society.

10

This way of thinking about post-war society was not, of course, confined to industrial society theorists. The idea that post-war western societies were, in an important sense 'post-capitalist' was much more widely shared. For many, the trade-cycle, as well as the class war, belonged to another age – one that had been left behind as better methods of managing a complex technological society had been found. Furthermore, it was claimed that a corporate economy was different from the classical competitive market economy: it entailed managed markets and a separation of control from ownership. Corporate management therefore enjoyed a good deal of freedom from the old-style constraints of profit maximisation.

The doctrine of 'managerial revolution' and cognate theses of post-capitalism – so much in vogue in the 1950s and 1960s – are well known, and need no elaboration.[29] They are mentioned here to emphasise the wide currency that the idea of a 'post-capitalist' or industrial society enjoyed in the post-war years. Within this perspective post-war western society appeared as qualitatively different from the society of pre-war days. At the same time its new features appeared as 'evolutionary' and irreversible. Implicitly or explicitly the welfare state was seen as a part of this change. At once necessary and beneficial, it formed an integral part of the evolutionary development of western industrial societies.[30]

True, there were other theoretical approaches to modern society which did not take the welfare state entirely for granted. For example the citizenship view associated with T. H. Marshall saw some potential for conflict between the values of welfare and those of market capitalism.[31] Moreover, social democratic thinkers, notably Titmuss, rejected deterministic theories such as industrialism and convergence altogether. Social welfare policy involved value conflict and choice and there was no immanent social principle making for an automatic consensus.[32] All the same, the Titmussian approach came down firmly on the side of the welfare state. Indeed it seemed to have virtually equated the welfare state with the good society itself so that the only problem was that there was not enough social welfare. For this school, too, no functional incompatibility was involved between market capitalism and welfare. Society had the right, and indeed the duty – a moral obligation – to choose between competing values. These value choices implied different ways of doing things, for example, private medicine or the NHS, private pension plans or state pensions, from which different consequences followed regarding individual welfare and the quality of social life. For Titmuss and other Fabians, with their strong penchant for state collectivism, the social services fostered the sense of community and helped to create one society. They therefore saw social welfare in integrative terms and, on the whole, ignored the possibility that the state welfare system could give rise to dysfunctions.[33]

In any case it seemed obvious in the 1950s and 1960s that the welfare state was doing no harm, and perhaps much good, to the market economy and capitalism. The debate on welfare therefore focused on distribution taking production – a more or less steady growth in national output – for granted. Even Marxism, the most venerable theory of conflicts and contradictions, faced with the apparent success of welfare capitalism, tended to see social welfare in positively functional terms. If industrial society theorists saw the welfare state as functional for the industrial order, Marxists saw it as functional for a capitalist social order.[34] For Marxists, too, the welfare state represented, more or less, a logical development of capitalism to a stage where the state must play a prominent part in managing the economy (accumulation) and offering concessions to the oppressed majority (legitimisation).[35] True, Marxism also included a theory of class conflict and societal contradictions, but until quite recently Marxist analysis of the state has tended to emphasise its positive functions for capitalism. All in all, the welfare state took on a necessary and inevitable character in post-war social theory.

The promise of a social 'science'
Quite apart from the influence of broad gauge theories such as functionalism and industrialism, there was one other intellectual development which helped to legitimise the post-war welfare and the idea of social intervention and social engineering more generally. This was the promise of a social 'science'. It was more a promise than an accomplished fact, for in stark contrast with the natural sciences and technology – highly

advanced in their knowledge base – the social field was characterised by the absence of reliable knowledge. However, the success of post-war economic reconstruction, influenced by Keynesian thinking lent credence to the idea that at least economics might be coming of age as a 'science'.[36] And it was clear by the early 1960s that economics had developed a range of reliable techniques – backed by sophisticated theories and quantifiable models – for managing the economy. There was no reason why it should not travel further along the road of science. Other social disciplines, for example, sociology and psychology, it was believed, could emulate economics and in due course emerge as sciences, and generate well-tested theories which would enable social phenomena to be understood and controlled with scientific precision.

Moreover, central to the idea of an advanced industrial society is cognitive knowledge – above all scientific knowledge – and the mastery of the natural world through its systematic application. Social knowledge, in parallel with the knowledge produced by physical and biomedical sciences, was seen as a part of this advanced social order. The prosperity of post-war years provided the wherewithal for a vast expansion in higher education. The same conditions also favoured investment in research and development, under public as well as private auspices. The spectacular growth of the social sciences in the 1960s attested to the willingness of society to underwrite the development of social knowledge as well as the hopes pinned on it. No one can doubt the seriousness with which the idea of a major breakthrough in social knowledge was taken in those days and disciplines such as sociology believed themselves to be on the brink of founding a science of society. Moreover, it is no coincidence that it was in the United States – modern, highly industrial, and searching for useful social know-how – that the idea of a social science was taken really seriously. The new discipline of sociology, especially in its scientistic orientation, found far greater acceptance in the US than in the less technocratic milieu of Western Europe.

The advancement of the social sciences promised better understanding of social problems and their solution. This encouraged the belief that social engineering – whether undertaken by the state or other agencies – would succeed in the

13

same way that industrial technology and economic management seemed to be succeeding in their own spheres. Western Europe, given its evolution out of a pre-modern culture and its deep-rooted ideological conflicts, has been far less positivistic in its outlook than North America. Europe has therefore been somewhat less enamoured of the idea of a social science and technology. Not so the United States. For the USA the War on Poverty and the war in Vietnam were in a sense similar operations. Vast resources were committed to both, and the 'intelligence' of an industrial society mobilised to ensure success. The poverty problem was to be tackled in a systematic, scientific way much like industrial and military problems – and with the same success. The full resources of the 'new' social science were to be mobilised to put the Great Society into orbit.[37] No wonder disenchantment with social science, with its promise to solve social problems and deliver 'welfare' in an apolitical and scientised manner, appears to have been so pronounced in the United States.[38] In Europe, ever since the days of Bismarck, the welfare state has been seen largely in political and ideological terms. Social policy has been more an exercise in statecraft than in social technology. Looked at from another angle, it has appeared as a matter of choice based on social values. Neither social issues nor their resolution has been seen primarily in technical terms, so less was expected of social science and consequently the sense of disappointment with the social sciences, at least in relation to social policy, has been much less.

However, let us not exaggerate the difference between Europe and North America in this respect. For the truth is that in the 1960s, the belief was current throughout the West that the foundations of a science of society were at last being laid and that armed with this knowledge society would be able to manage its affairs far more successfully. State intervention in economic and social matters was not only legitimate politically but also intellectually. Economics as well as other fledgeling social sciences held out the promise that society could manage its affairs 'rationally' rather than leave them to chance, to *laisser-faire*, to the operation of the market, to drift. This social rationality – like its counterpart in industrial man's dealings with nature – was after all one aspect of the rationalisation of the modern world so ponderously reflected upon by Weber.[39] Since economic and social *laisser-faire* had brought western societies to the verge of collapse in the 1930s, it seemed perverse not to try to produce knowledge and to use it for a better understanding and management of social life.

Western social science, furthermore, saw the issue of social planning and intervention largely in terms of 'piecemeal social engineering'.[40] What was required was not wholesale planning and recasting of the social organisation, but the correction and investigation of specific evils. And this, more or less, was what the welfare state stood for. It intended leaving much of society, including the market economy, as self-regulating while ironing out some of the instability and imbalances through judicious piecemeal intervention. This was nothing new. Reformers had been tackling evils piecemeal since the beginning of industrial-isation and urbanisation in the nineteenth century. Social legislation – factory reform, workmen's compensation, social insurance and a host of other measures – had already institutionalised this pattern of development. The post-war welfare state made the process more systematic, gave it a clearer rationale, and at the same time extended the scope of state action a good deal. Social science meanwhile held out the promise that this task could be put on a firmer, scientific footing.

The name Karl Popper is not one that usually comes to mind in connection with social reform. Yet perhaps the intellectual, as well as social, justification for 'piecemeal social engineering' has been provided most eloquently by Popper, a leading philosopher of scientific method.[41] Decrying attempts at large-scale and utopian societal change, Popper argued strongly in favour of tackling social evils piecemeal. A small, well-defined problem was much more amenable to alleviation through social measures than some abstract, vaguely defined ill. Piecemeal social engineering, claimed Popper, allowed far greater scope for controlling variables and ascertaining the effect of a particular measure than the attempt to change society wholesale – as Marxists and other utopians wished to do.[42] Such piecemeal social reforms were, of course, to be carried out by the state. A philosopher of freedom and the 'Open Society', Popper was not averse to state intervention. In this respect he sided with the social liberalism of the post-war years rather than with the radical libertarianism of Hayek. For Hayek state collectivism was the road to serfdom.[43] By contrast, for Popper, reform through judicious, small-scale state intervention was the method by which a liberal society progressed. The answer to the utopianism preached by Marxists was not *laisser-faire* but state intervention. If we 'wish freedom to be safeguarded', he wrote, 'then we must demand that the policy of unlimited economic freedom be replaced by the planned economic intervention of the state. We must demand that unrestrained capitalism give way to an economic interventionism. And this is precisely what has happened.'[44] In short, social science knowledge and piecemeal social engineering were to keep western societies free, liberal as well as progressive, and this was to be the task of the welfare state.

Socialism through welfare

A rather different, but none the less important, source of support for the post-war welfare state has been its association with socialism. For progressive conservatives and liberals state intervention was a form of meliorism which helped to make individual freedom and the market society more secure. For parliamentary socialists, on the other hand, state action had far greater potential. Socialist governments could use state power to create a more egalitarian society through peaceful, constitutional means. To many social democrats, western industrial society in the 1950s seemed increasingly 'post-capitalist' and the nationalisation of the means of production no longer seemed relevant to socialism. It was argued that through a variety of policies – fiscal, industrial and social – the state could exercise indirect control over the market economy. Leaving production largely in private hands the state could socialise distribution and thus go a long way towards achieving the egalitarian objectives of socialism. The development of social services and other collective amenities on the one hand and the equalisation of incomes through progressive taxation on the other could lead society toward socialism. In this perspective the welfare state became a 'part-way' house to socialism. As Crosland put it, 'the planned full employment welfare state, which has been the outcome of the first successful spell of Labour government, is a society of exceptional merit and quality by historical standards . . . It would have seemed a paradise to many early socialist pioneers;.'[45] Crosland went on to observe that while the welfare state did meet some of the socialist aspirations it could be 'a great deal more socialist than it is.'[46] And this had little to do with extending public ownership or embarking on detailed economic planning – such means were unnecessary for achieving socialist objectives. Rather it was a matter of realising traditional socialist aims through the existing political and economic institutions. In short, the socialist objective was greater social equality and it could be achieved through the managed economy and social welfare.[47]

Indeed, once post-war social democracy had downgraded nationalisation as a means to socialism it was left primarily with welfarism (in some form or another) as the means to a more compassionate, just and equal society. Perhaps Sweden epitomises what was best in this notion of 'welfare socialism'. At any rate, the belief in realising socialist objectives through state action – equality of opportunity in education, comprehensive schooling, universal social services, and the like – gave the pursuit of social welfare a legitimacy in the eyes of the Labourites and socialists which differed from that of liberals such as Beveridge. For the latter, the rationale of state action was to make a liberal market society more stable, efficient and humane. For socialists state action was a means of transforming society – of changing it gradually, bit by bit, from capitalism to a form of socialism. The method was piecemeal social engineering, but the result was seen in cumulative terms.[48]

The various assumptions underlying this notion of change cannot be examined here, although some of these will already be familiar to students of welfare.[49] Suffice to note at this stage that welfare socialism was also based on the idea of a positively functional, or at any rate neutral, relationship between the welfare state and the market economy. The conflict between the market and welfare was primarily at the level of values. Focusing largely on distribution and social stratification, welfare socialism took the productive system of capitalism for granted. Relying on Keynesian notions of the mixed economy and its management, it discounted the possibility that changes in the pattern of distribution or the growth of social expenditure might affect economic production adversely. More generally, faith in 'rational' action, through the medium of parliamentary politics and government and in the process of cumulative, irreversible reform inclined socialists towards 'eager collectivism'.[50]

It is true that the idea of the welfare state held by moderate ('reluctant') collectivists like Beveridge and Keynes was quite different from that of eager collectivists like Titmuss and Crosland. Both the nature and the scope of state action envisaged was different. But two things at least were common to these different approaches. First, was a belief in the state's ability to manage economic and social affairs rationally. This entailed a trust in the state's neutrality as well as its effectiveness in carrying out the tasks laid upon it by parliament. We may call this the belief in the administrative or bureaucratic rationality of the modern state. This view of rationality discounted the idea that government action might have unintended consequences, or that state institutions could become the vehicle of sectional interests. Secondly, common to both reluctant and eager collectivists, was the belief that the welfare state would help, or at least not hinder, the market economy and the system of production more generally. This might be described as a belief in pragmatism, or in the method of piecemeal social engineering. To a large extent the current crisis of legitimacy concerns the validity of these two assumptions.

The Receding Tide

We have identified a set of factors, some material others ideological, which gave legitimacy to the post-war welfare state: a buoyant economy, the Keynes – Beveridge rationale for state intervention, theories of industrial society and post-capitalism, the promise of a science of society, and the pursuit of socialism through welfare. By the end of the 1970s, most of these supports had been seriously weakened.

First and foremost, the steady economic growth of the earlier decades has given way to economic stagnation accompanied by high rates of inflation. From time to time, stagflation threatens to turn into slumpflation. Overall, the western economy is in recession. Unemployment has been rising almost everywhere. The presence of recession and inflation at the same time has confounded Keynesian economics and has led to a collapse of confidence in the state's ability to manage a mixed economy. The problems that have arisen are material as much as ideational: material in that the affluence of the early post-war decades enabled social expenditure to be financed, more or less, out of the growing social dividend. Now the economic base is static, or even shrinking. Governments are faced with mounting deficits and the prospect of retrenching social expenditure. The alternative is higher taxation – an unpopular measure at the best of times and more so in times of economic difficulty. The ideational aspect of the problem is no less serious. The entire Keynesian approach, which legitimised certain kinds of state intervention for regulating demand and maintaining full employment, now stands discredited.[51] The economic rationale of the welfare state has been weakened seriously, leaving only the social or Beveridgian aspects in place. And these, by and large, now seem to form the principal justification for state welfare provision. The contribution of income maintenance, health care and other social programmes towards social integration – sustaining minimal standards and thus helping to maintain social peace and the idea of a national community – remains the single most important prop for the welfare state. Indeed, with rising unemployment this shock-absorber function of social welfare has become more evident.

The Keynes – Beveridge package of welfare implied that state policies would sustain both economic well-being (full employment and economic growth) and social welfare. With the eclipse of Keynesianism, the social has been cut loose from the economic and the two seem to be drifting apart. Increasingly, social expenditure and social welfare more generally are seen as having adverse consequences on the economy. At least one school of thought (see Chapter 2) blames inflation and the recession squarely on the growth of government. Its answer to the economic ills of the West is to roll back the frontiers of the state, reduce taxes and restore the dynamism of the private sector. Social welfare, from this viewpoint, blocks the way to economic recovery and a prosperous market economy.

Functionalist theories of society – industrialism, convergence, modernisation – went into decline in the early 1970s well before the onset of stagflation and the demise of Keynesianism.[52] By the early 1970s capitalism had been rediscovered in practice as well as in theory. In the face of persistent class privilege and inequality in advanced societies, the war in Vietnam and the continuing exploitation and underdevelopent of the Third World, theories of post-capitalism and modernisation began to look increasingly threadbare. Student rebellions of the late 1960s and the 'events' of May 1968 in France spelled the end of the 'end of ideology' thesis associated with these theories. Marxist theory seemed to offer a far better purchase on contemporary reality, and interest in Marxist social science revived throughout the West. From a different perspective, a growing body of scholarly literature began to cast serious doubt on the validity of the thesis of convergence and the underlying notion of technological determinism.[53] It drew attention to the plurality of influences in social development and to its uneven and discontinuous nature. It emphasised the role of politics, ideology and choice in social affairs. As a result, the idea of the welfare state as an inevitable product of industrialisation and modernity began to look less plausible. More generally, the theses connected with post-capitalism – managerial revolution, decreasing significance of social class, plural distribution of power in western societies – came under heavy critical fire from social scientists of the Left.[54] The upshot was that by the mid-1970s the image of post-war society as a smoothly evolving industrial social order, in important and irreversible ways 'post-capitalist', was badly tarnished. What credibility was still left in the theories of industrialism and post-capitalism has been undermined seriously by the economic recession and the mounting problems of welfare capitalism. The optimistic, evolutionary scenario consisting of affluent industrialism and the welfare state has disappeared leaving the future of the western societies looking uncertain and unpredictable.[55]

By the beginning of the 1980s, little was left of the promise of a 'science' of society. Economics, which was believed to have come of age as a social science, is itself in deep trouble. Keynesiansim is in disarray and the neo-classical theories of market have made a comeback.[56] Yet, in so far as monetarism and the supply side economics (see Chapter 2) have been tried – in Britain and the USA – the results have been disappointing. Economics finds itself without a theory that can explain the conundrum of slumpflation and show the way out. Ingenious arguments and sophisticated techniques abound but cannot make up for the absence of a reliable theoretical paradigm.

But long before economics proved to be an emperor without clothes, sociology and the social sciences more broadly conceived were found wanting as reliable guides to action. By the late 1960s many social commentators and policy analysts in the United States were finding the results of War on Poverty and other Great Society programmes disappointing (see pp. 31-4, 39 below). Much effort and expenditure had gone into these but with only meagre results. Social scientists' own evaluations of these programmes were conflicting and no one really knew what was their outcome. To solve the age-old problem of poverty, dependency, deviance and the like, Congress, and the American political leadership more generally, had pinned their hopes on social science, but the social scientists had failed to deliver. On the whole, the anti-poverty programmes had revealed the poverty of social engineering. The gap between promise and performance was too wide to be ignored.

Clearly in the absence of a reliable science and technology of society social policy could not be rational, but remained a hit-or-miss affair. Piecemeal social engineering – *ad hoc* tinkering with social problems – had unforeseen effects which created new problems elsewhere in the social system. The idea that planned social action under the auspices of the state (Popper's 'interventionism' and 'social engineering') could be used to manage social affairs effectively had proved unrealistic. Government failure seemed no less serious than market failure, and many neo-conservatives in the United States (and elsewhere) drew the conclusion that state intervention was doing more harm than good (see pp. 31-6 below). And quite apart from social engineering, it had become evident by the mid-1970s that the idea of a 'science' of society (similar to the natural sciences) was premature, if not altogether unrealistic.[57] True, much useful social knowledge had been produced – sociology, politics and other disciplines had expanded the frontiers of social thought and awareness a great deal. On the whole they seemed to play an indispensable part in providing society with self-knowledge. But this social awareness was a far cry from the idea of 'laws', 'prediction' and demonstrably effective techniques of control believed at one time to be within the grasp of the social disciplines. Clearly, to admit the failure of the social sciences in this sense is to admit that the knowledge-base which would make rational action through the state possible is lacking. Hence the force of the neo-conservative argument that the limitations of social knowledge also indicate the limits of social policy. But quite apart from neo-conservatism, the awareness that social phenomena are exceedingly complex and that social knowledge remains uncertain has weakened the rationale for government action in economic and social affairs.

The social democratic belief that socialist objectives could be pursued through parliamentary means, and above all through welfare policies, had looked most convincing in the 1950s. In Britain, for example, the Labour government returned to power immediately after the second world war had carried out quite extensive reforms which were seen as pushing Britain towards socialism.[58] There was no reason why the next Labour government could not carry out another round of social reforms. Since popular reforms could not be reversed easily, the cumulative impact of these changes, it was believed, would be to bring society closer to the socialist goal. The welfare state was to play a major part in this process of transformation.

But while doubt about such an easy route to socialism had already begun by the late 1950s,[59] at least another decade was to pass before welfare socialism would begin to lose its credibility. The 'rediscovery' of poverty, and the persistent inequality in the distribution of income and wealth, showed that the levelling effects of affluence, universal social services and progressive taxation had been grossly exaggerated. Moreover, it appeared that market forces were able to counteract the effect of egalitarian policies (for example, progressive taxation) quite successfully (for example, through fringe benefits). However, such findings did not, at first, question seriously the strategy of welfare socialism. The implication was, rather, that the extent of change had been exaggerated and the obstacles on the road to equality had been underestimated. What was required, therefore, was a more determined effort to bring about change in the light of better knowledge about social facts.[60] Yet successive Labour governments failed to make much difference to the situation.[61] In this, Britain was not unique. Other social democratic countries also showed persistent inequalities, notably in the distribution of income and wealth.[62] Social expenditure had risen as a proportion of GNP in all western countries and in some the rise was quite impressive. But social welfare, it turned out, was not redistributing resources from the rich to the poor. Rather, it was a system of horizontal redistribution which involved intra-class rather than inter-class transfers. Overall, the system of taxation was scarcely progressive while the universality of the social services meant that they benefited rich and poor alike. Faced with such evidence, some socialists persisted in the belief that, given the will and the right strategy, much more could be accomplished. Others however began to question the validity of the basic assumptions underlying welfare socialism.

If the early 1960s rediscovered poverty, the late 1960s both rediscovered capitalism and saw the revival of Marxism. Intellectually, western Marxism was slowly freeing itself from the dead hand of Stalinist orthodoxy and, by the late 1960s, was beginning to come to terms with the phenomena of liberal politics and the welfare state.[63] Marxist analysis of the state and the nature of power in post-war western societies, reinforcing that of non-Marxist radicals, began to challenge pluralist conceptions of the liberal polity including the state. Above all, a Marxist interpretation of the nature of the capitalist state also explained the limits of social policy and reform. The welfare state was not paving the way to socialism, rather in western societies the state, whether with a little more welfare provision or less, remained in the service of capital and the ruling class. Hence, argued Marxists and other radicals, the idea of bringing about structural change through the agency of the liberal state was quite unrealistic.[64] The Left critique thus drew attention to the limited space within which the welfare state was operating and was, so to speak, condemned to operate. Not only had it failed to achieve significant re-distribution of income and opportunity it could not even eliminate poverty. Moreover, given the nature of the social system of which it was a part it was unlikely to do so.[65]. From the standpoint of the radical Left the welfare state appeared, in effect as a vast confidence trick, an ideological apparatus in the service of capitalism rather than a social system in the transition to socialism. The slumpflation of the 1970s has clearly underlined the unrealism of a socialist strategy based on manipulating distribution while leaving production in capitalist hands. Mass unemployment, cutbacks in social expenditure and tax concessions to the rich are a harsh reminder that 'welfare' is only tolerable so long as it does not interfere with the logic of capitalist production. The choice seems to be between capitalism and welfare capitalism. Pursuit of socialism through welfare has proved to be a myth.

The issues we have raised do not by any means exhaust the problem of legitimacy facing the welfare state. Among others we could mention professional and bureaucratic vested interests, efficiency and cost-effectiveness in public services, and patriarchal ideology and practices in the state welfare services. The first two issues are related to the notion of government failure and are discussed in that context in Chapter 2. Little, however, will be said about 'anarchistic' ideologies of welfare which oppose the professional-bureaucratic state organisation and favour voluntarism, de-bureaucratisation, self-care, community action, and the like. As regards sexism, let us note first of all that, on the whole, feminists do not reject the welfare state as such,[66] rather they wish to change its patriarchal nature and make it more equitable for women. This may be seen largely as a plea against discrimination, but it is also clear that equal treatment of the sexes in the context of welfare involves quite far-reaching changes in social organisation. This, however, raises the problem of sexual stratification in society – a problem, like race and class, too large to be considered within the confines of this book.

To sum up: the broad consensus concerning the mixed economy and the welfare state so characteristic of western societies since the second world war has weakened a good deal in recent years. The welfare state is faced with a crisis of legitimacy. As Keynesianism and other social theories of the Centre, which served either as a practical guide to state intervention or as its intellectual underpinning, have lost credibility the radical critique of welfare, from the Right as well as the Left, has gained ascendancy. The arguments advanced from the two ends of the spectrum of social thought – paradoxically they also share certain orientations and analyses – have acquired greater plausibility.

The characteristic mood, however, remains one of intellectual uncertainty. As far as social (including economic and political) phenomena are concerned, western countries seem to be without a reliable compass. The ideas of the Right have gained ground and have been put into practice in some countries, notably the UK and the USA. It is most unlikely that these experiments – quite apart from their cost in privation and suffering – will succeed in reviving economic growth (see pp. 46-53 below). What if they fail? Where will the politicians turn next? Not only the future of the welfare state but also that of the liberal polity and the market economy remains uncertain. Those of us involved in the study of social policy and welfare must try to come to grips with this crisis. Policy analysis can no longer take the parameters of the welfare state for granted. Whatever is happening in our backyards, on our doorsteps – and what *will* be happening in the coming months and years – cannot be understood without a grasp of the wider problems besetting the welfare state. That, indeed, is the rationale of this book. The issues raised in this chapter are taken up in the context of a number of more or less distinct ideological orientations to the present crisis examined in the following four chapters. The final chapter outlines some of the practical and theoretical implications of the analysis offered in the preceding chapters.

2   Forward to *Laisser-Faire*: the new Right

It was pointed out in the last chapter that despite a broad consensus over the welfare state there was also, since its inception, a small but strident Right which rejected the market-state mix represented by the post-war settlement. Instead, it proclaimed its faith in the classical doctrines of the market and individualism, and deplored the compromise between capitalism and socialism represented by the new middle course. Economists such as Hayek and Friedman, for example, have espoused these views for many years. The basic arguments and value premises of the anti-collectivists hardly need rehearsing.[1] The doctrine of economic and social *laisser-faire* has, after all, been the reigning orthodoxy in English-speaking countries for the best part of their modern history. In the literature of social policy this doctrine has been enshrined in the 'residual' model of welfare in which the role of the state is largely confined to relieving the hard core of proverty.[2] In the wake of the Great Depression and the miseries it inflicted on the populace, the successful management of the economy during the war years by the government, and the rise of Keynesian doctrines, which legitimised state intervention and mixed economy, extreme anti-collectivism seemed increasingly like a voice from the past, irrelevant and anachronistic in the conditions of the post-war world. True, many of the values and beliefs held by the anti-collectivists resonated well with what was essentially a capitalist society. But in its pristine form their doctrine found few followers. Moreover, the social policy entailed by the anti-collectivist doctrine was not considered practical by even the most conservative of politicians. All the same, it should be remembered that Keynesian economics, including the policy of full employment, did not find ready

acceptance in capitalist circles, nor did the idea of a comprehensive welfare state. What was decisive, however, in establishing a *de facto* consensus over the mixed economy and the
welfare state was the long economic 'boom' and the apparent
success and popularity of the welfare state. These conditions
offered little scope for the doctrines of the Right to attain a
sympathetic hearing let alone widespread following.

The 1970s changed all that. In the face of persistent stagflation Keynesianism has virtually collapsed as a theory and as
a guide to action, and the resulting vacuum has promptly been
filled by theories of the Right (and, in a different sense, of the
Left). After waiting for years in the wings they have suddenly
moved into the limelight. At last, notes an exultant Friedman,
'The tide is turning' away from Fabian socialism and New
Deal liberalism towards greater freedom and limited government. The collectivist trend which

has now lasted three-quarters of a century in Britain, half a century in
the United States . . . is cresting. Its intellectual basis has been eroded
as experience has repeatedly contradicted expectations. Its sup-
porters are on the defensive. They have no solutions to offer to
present-day evils except more of the same. They can no longer arouse
enthusiasm among the young who now find the ideas of Adam Smith
or Karl Marx far more exciting than Fabian socialism or New Deal
liberalism.[3]

This is no mere rhetoric. Within the last decade or so a neo-
conservative movement in social thought has emerged that
goes well beyond the confines of economic *laisser-faire*, namely,
faith in monetarism and the free-play of market forces. Indeed it
is no exaggeration to speak of a neo-conservative counter-
revolution in social thought, even if it is largely centred in the
United States.[4]

This Rightist revival is not simply an assertion of the old
doctrines in circumstances more congenial to their reception.
Naturally there is a great deal of continuity with the classical
doctrines of individualism and *laisser-faire* which, for example, can be traced back in economics to Adam Smith and in
sociology to Herbert Spencer. But there is also a good deal that
is new, for example, a variety of arguments related to the
experience of state intervention in liberal market societies

during the post-war decades. The negative record (or at least evaluation) of Soviet-style socialism also plays a part, albeit indirect, in giving neo-conservatism its panache and confidence.[5] It would certainly not do to dismiss this current of thought lightly. The arguments put forward are economic, sociological as well as philosophical. While some of this, notably the economic argument, is of the 'I told you so' variety, taken together the ideas of the new Right represent a significant counter-thrust against social democracy and liberalism – the ideological props of the welfare state – and against the Left more generally. Paradoxically however the radical Left and the radical Right also share many ideas and analyses regarding the current situation.[6]

But if the 1970s began with an upsurge of Marxist social thought, they have closed with a recrudescence of conservatism. Be that as it may, the neo-conservatives offer what, on the face of it, looks like a coherent and plausible analysis of the current problems besetting welfare capitalism as well as a set of prescriptions for their solution. It is necessary to look at these in some detail. However within the confines of a single chapter we can scarcely present, let alone examine systematically, the different economic, philosophical and sociological strands of the neo-conservative argument. Rather we shall be concerned with the broad intellectual argument, especially in its sociological and economic aspects, and its tentative appraisal.

Government Growth

For social democrats, progressive liberals and even for Marxists the growth of government in the post-war years appears as a 'rational' phenomenon, in the sense of having a clear rationale – a development deliberately undertaken to attain certain ends. For Marxists, the capitalist state expands in order to perform such necessary functions as accumulation and legitimisation. For social democrats and liberals it represents a a growing recognition of collective responsibility for the economic and social well-being of the nation. For the conservatives, on the other hand, the post-war welfare state represents an unprincipled, excessive and harmful government growth. From the idea that it is proper for the government to regulate the market economy and provide economic security for the population (the Keynes–Beveridge package of modest collectivism) it is a short step to the government taking over responsibility for every sort of economic and social ill. As Kristol writes:

the welfare state, over the past twenty-five years, lost its original self-definition and became something more ambitious, more inflated, and incredibly more expensive. It became the paternalistic state, addressing itself to every variety of 'problem' and committed to 'solving' them all – committed, that is, to making human life unproblematic.[7]

On the other side of the Atlantic, King writes in a similar vein about government growth:

[The] range of matters for which British governments hold themselves responsible – and for which they believe that the electorate may hold them responsible – has increased greatly over the past ten or twenty years . . . and is still increasing at a rapid rate. So rapid is the rate indeed that most of us, although aware of it, have become insensitive to it, just as citizens of certain countries have become inured to comparable rates of price inflation.[8]

Nowadays there is 'hardly anything in which government can avoid taking an interest. [and] . . . [T]o be held responsible for everything is to feel compelled to intervene in everything.'[9] This heightened sense of government responsibility has nothing, however, to do with social conscience or other such altruistic social principles, rather it is electoral pressure and expediency of competitive democratic politics that has pushed governments further and further into becoming 'responsible' for everything.

That the 'political market' is largely responsible for government growth is an important part of the neo-conservative argument. Very briefly, it is argued that behaviour in the world of democratic, competitive politics is best understood in terms broadly similar to behaviour in the market economy.[10] Thus political parties compete with one another for the popular vote rather like businesses competing for customers. Politicians' promises, if voted to power, are made somewhat in the manner of businesses' claims for their products. The political market however also differs in important ways from the economic market. For example, in the former the discipline of resource constraint and the price tag is missing. In these circumstances, electoral competition encourages excessive expectations of government; it socialises the electorate into making unconscionable demands on the government.[11] Theorists of the political market concede the role of political ideology in restraining this competitive bidding for votes, but also believe that the 'vote motive' pushes mass political parties towards pragmatism and ideological convergence.[12] According to these theorists, parties formulate policies in order to win elections rather than the other way round. Ideology is not unimportant, but in conditions of electoral politics it functions chiefly as a weapon in the fight for office.[13] Party politics then leads, indirectly, to government growth and to heightened expectations on the part of the electorate.

But that is not all. Organised interest groups constantly articulate demands which, for competitive reasons, governments and political parties find difficult to ignore. Furthermore, special interest groups, whether seeking government subsidy, protection from foreign competition or help for a particular disadvantaged group, work singlemindedly to achieve what they want. And whilst the majority of the electorate, as individuals, may be in favour of market principles and limited government, most organised groups 'wish an exception to be made in their favour.'[14] The result is that organised interests and lobbies succeed in expanding the frontiers of government in a way that no one really intended. Moreover political wheeling and dealing (e.g. log-rolling politics in the United States where a vote in support for one project is traded for another) often has the same effect. In this way, the scope of government action as well as the budget expands far beyond that desired by the electorate without anyone consciously willing it.[15]

Among other pressures towards government growth conservatives single out the state bureaucracy itself. Far from being a mere servant of the public or an obedient tool of the politician the bureaucracy is a sectional interest in its own right. Public bureaucracies, which work outside the constraints of cost-efficiency and competition, have an inherent tendency to grow. Market economists have elaborated sophisticated analyses of bureaucratic behaviour which, in essence, claim that just as businessmen seek to maximise profit, bureaucrats seek to maximise the size of their bureau.[16] For it is on the size and growth of the bureau that the advancement of status, salary and power of the bureaucracy depends. There is therefore an in-built 'law' of bureaucratic growth: as the scope of government activity expands so does the bureaucracy which interposes itself between the citizenry and their representatives. It becomes both a vehicle whereby special interests can achieve their objectives and an important special interest in its own right.[17] With growing size, the public services, comprising millions of state employees, professionals and others, come to serve those who work in them more than the consumer. Hence, claims Friedman, once government programmes and organisations are instituted they can rarely be dismantled. Rather, special interests press for their expansion, 'foremost among them the massive bureaucracy spawned by the programs'.[18] Moreover it is virtually impossible to control bureaucracies from outside because they have far greater knowledge of their own operations than politicians or other outside agencies can hope to possess. There is therefore a 'ratchet effect' which works against attempts to reduce government size.[19]

Government Failure

How far have governments succeeded in attaining various policy objectives? Has the massive growth in government and in public expenditure brought commensurate results? The neo-conservative answer to these questions is a clear no. Thus Friedman speaks of 'widespread dissatisfaction' with the results of the 'explosion in welfare activities' in the United States.[20] Neo-conservatives, some of whom have been closely involved with policy-making and analysis in the United States, are unanimous in the view that the War on Poverty and the Great Society programmes of the 1960s have been a failure.

Wildavsky speaks of 'an awful lot of money' having been invested 'without accomplishing much'.[21] 'The modern state', writes Moynihan, 'was getting into activities no one understood very well. It had not reached the point of picking every man a wife, but it was getting close enough to other such imponderables.'[22] Among such activities Moynihan includes various 'social initiatives designed to put an end to racial and ethnic discrimination, to poverty, and even also to unequal levels of achievement between various social groups.'[23] Kristol finds the 'skyrocketing costs of the welfare state' way out of line 'with its modest (if undubitable) benefits'.[24] King makes sweeping claims of government failure in one area after another in Britain: higher education, incomes policy, local government re-organisation. Many other areas of government activity tell the same story. Much, for example, was expected from higher education in promoting economic growth, social egalitarianism, and the like in the early 1960s. Ten years later not only was it clear that none of these things had happened but nobody seemed to know any longer what the objectives of higher education really were. Nobody knew how to produce a successful incomes policy even though a great deal of the nation's time and energy had been spent on it. Administrative re-organisation, of local government in the 1960s, and the NHS in the 1970s, had cost the nation a good deal but the benefits were hardly discernible.[25]

The idea of government failure is central to neo-conservative evaluation of the post-war state in general, and the welfare state in particular. The 'externalities' or the unforeseen and unintended consequences of government action constitute an important source of government failure. In this respect government failure is seen as paralleling market failure. Both types of action give rise to unforeseen – perhaps unforeseeable – side-effects. In some ways this is a new and formidable weapon in the hands of the new Right. If government action also leads to unforeseen and untoward consequences then the very idea of correcting market failure through government action is fatally flawed. Thus Friedman takes Galbraith to task for failing to analyse the externalities of government action and dwelling chiefly on forms of market failure. Friedman urges political scientists and sociologists who advocate government action to study its imperfections: 'Evidence that markets are imperfect does not create a case for government action, which may be even more imperfect.'[26] Aaron speaks of the 'collapse of that bubble of faith that government action is a force for good.'[27] By the time of the Watergate revelations 'the vague residual presumption that government actions could be guided to benign purposes by dedicated leaders was utterly obliterated.'[28] Wildavsky, a leading analyst of public policy in the United States, ruminates in sombre mood over the disappointed hopes and lost illusions of an earlier decade. Because of unanticipated consequences the solutions to social problems themselves become problems faster than social scientists' understanding can cope. 'We may be smart', observes Wildavsky wrily, 'but life is smarter.'[29]

Thus neo-conservatives claim that the liberalisation of welfare assistance helped push up the rate of family disorganisation among poor blacks in America. This is the opposite of what was expected. According to Kristol, 'something appears to have gone wrong: a liberal and compassionate social policy has bred all sorts of unanticipated and perverse consequences.'[30] One of the most important of these is 'the disorganisation and demoralisation of the negro family'.[31] Gilder, whose widely acclaimed *Wealth and Poverty* may be described as a hymn to free-enterprise capitalism, goes much further than these neo-conservatives in describing the malign influence of welfare on the poor, and especially the black family. His diatribe against the demoralised poor, and against state assistance responsible for their plight, is reminiscent of the language of the Poor Law Report of 1834:

What actually happened since 1964 was a vast expansion of the welfare rolls that halted in its tracks an ongoing improvement in the life of the poor, particularly blacks and left behind . . . a wreckage of broken lives and families worse than the aftermath of slavery.[32]

Generous welfare assistance has led to an 'increasing reluctance of the American poor to perform low-wage labour.'[33] Above all, welfare was sapping the will to strive, to make an effort to get ahead. 'In order to succeed', writes Gilder with the fervour of a Victorian Poor Law reformer, 'the poor need most of all the spur of their poverty.'[34] In short, we are back to the 'less eligibility' principle of 1834. In the early 1970s, it was the radical social scientist such as Gans who, turning Parsonian functionalism on its head, wrote of the functions of poverty in capitalist America.[35] It is a sign of the changed times – of how far the conservative mood pervades the United States – that an apologist of free-enterprise capitalism proudly proclaims the necessity of poverty in a capitalist society, a necessity which the welfare system fails to appreciate.

A somewhat more abstract and sophisticated catalogue of social policy failure is provided by Glazer. For Glazer too the failure is due, in part, to unintended consequences. First, he notes, social policy which attempts to deal with the breakdown of traditional ways of handling distress itself leads to a further weakening of the structures of the family, the ethnic group, the neighbourhood, the Church, etc. The result is greater dependence on the government, and the need for further social policy. Paradoxically, then, 'our efforts to deal with distress themselves increase distress.'[36] Secondly, social policy (government intervention in social arrangements) inevitably raises expectations. The promise of social policy 'inadequately realised, leaves behind a high level of expectation, which a new round of social policy must attempt to meet, and with the same consequence.'[37] Finally, social policy itself, in almost every field, creates new and unmanageable demands. For it is wrong to see social policy as simply a solution to a particular problem. Rather 'there are dynamic aspects to any policy, such that it also *expands* the problem, *changes* the problem, *generates* further problems.'[38] And so the process goes on leaving in its wake confusion, uncertainty and frustration.

Another source of government failure, according to the new Right, is the naive collectivist equation of the common good with state action. Collectivists believe that there is an identifiable 'public interest' and that once it is identified the agencies of the state can be relied on to act in a neutral way to further public interest. This assumption has proved quite unrealistic.[39] In fact, the social policy process is extremely complex. Thus, in respect of social objectives such as adequate income (prevention of poverty), medical care, education and the like, the ends are being continuously redefined by those responsible for the necessary services. In this process of definition, sectional

34

interests begin to take over under the cloak of public interest. This is an important argument in the neo-conservative attack on the 'rationality' of state action.

Interestingly enough, the conservative criticism of the state in this respect coincides with neo-Weberian critiques of functionalism and organisation theory. The common ground is methodological individualism in the analysis of social phenomena.[40] Thus what the new Right seems to be saying, in effect, is that to impute a clear, rational, logical function to the state is to reify a complex, ongoing interaction process. It is to forget that state institutions consist of a variety of actors in pursuit of their 'own' objectives which may have little to do with imputed goals of the organisation. Collectivists, such as Keynes and Beveridge, assumed a benevolent and disinterested bureaucracy. But the state and its institutions become the vehicle for furthering the private interests of public employees and others whose livelihood depends on the perpetuation and expansion of the government. Under the cloak of public interest, then, the government may in fact be serving private interest. In Friedman's graphic language:

In the government sphere, as in the market, there seems to be an invisible hand, but it operates in precisely the opposite direction from Adam Smith's: an individual who intends only to serve the public interest by fostering government intervention is 'led by an invisible hand to promote' private interests, 'which was no part of his intention'.[41]

It should perhaps be noted that by now the idea of the welfare sector as a constituency of the service workers and professionals has a wide currency going well beyond the neo-conservatives.[42] But it is the latter school of thought that has made it a weapon of attack on the welfare state. The main challenge posed by the new Right's argument to the collectivists is that the so-called 'general interest' is more often than not a mask for 'private interest'. How can the state, then, presume to act with benevolent neutrality, as a mere agent of the common good? In this sense, bureaucratic rationality turns out to be no less 'irrational' than market rationality. Taken together, the new Right's view of unprincipled government growth and government failure questions the assumption of the rationality of government implicit in the social democratic (the welfare state develops to meet various needs and its purpose and function more or less coincide) as well as the Marxist (the welfare state develops to meet the needs of capital-accumulation and legitimisation and its purpose and function roughly coincide) standpoints.

Government Overload

Closely related to the ideas of government growth and failure is that of government overload. Overload occurs when demands made on the government far exceed its capacity to meet them effectively. For some time now, the neo-conservatives claim, western democracies have been faced with a contradictory development. On the one hand, increasing demands have been placed on the government by various interest groups as well as by the electorate more generally. On the other hand, increasing democratisation has severely restricted government's capacity – its authority and freedom – to act. There is less compliance with authority all round. The population wants, indeed expects, government to control inflation, but government attempts to restrain groups through incomes policies, for example, do not work. Expectations run far ahead of what governments can deliver. There is therefore a stalemate – a more or less permanently frustrating situation. It has been referred to somewhat dramatically as the 'ungovernability of democracies'.[43]

In one sense it is a problem of authority and compliance; in another sense, a problem of consensus. By and large, the root of the problem is an 'excess' of egalitarianism and democracy. But the new Right points to a number of factors contributing directly to overload. First, the post-war years have seen a vast growth in organised interest groups. Society has become highly politicised and the organisational slack, which provided democratic governments with room to manoeuvre and accept new demands, has been much reduced. Second, during the same period there has been a virtual revolution of rising expectations or, better still, entitlements. The idea of social rights and entitlements, and the notion that it is the government's responsibility to underwrite these, has become widespread. Third, traditional restraints on the part of various groups have been gradually eroded. Sectional interest is being pressed to the full as notions of traditional income differentials, deference or other modes of restraint lose their influence. Fourth, social complexity has increased greatly, but social knowledge lags behind and cannot cope. As governments intervene in more and more areas of society, the limitations of social science become increasingly apparent.

The first two points are brought out well in the well-known report to the *Trilateral Commission* on the crisis of democracy.[44] The idea of government overload was central to this report concerned largely with the question of governability. The onset of economic recession underlined the seriousness of these issues and served as a warning that difficult times might be ahead politically. On the topical and serious problem of inflation the report commented: 'In the face of the claims of business groups, labour unions, and the beneficiaries of government largesse, it becomes difficult if not impossible for democratic governments to curtail spending, increase taxes, and control prices and wages.'[45] Domestic problems were becoming 'intractable'. While government activity and expenditure was growing in order to meet public demands, success of government in achieving its goal remained 'dubious'. According to the report, the rapid growth of government expenditure in the 1960s in western countries was far from a benign development. Governments had various responsibilities and functions thrust upon them by the populace. Thus government involvement was not so much a sign of strength as of weakness. Political leaders had proved unable and unwilling to

reject the demands made upon them [by various important groups in society] .... The democratic idea that government should be responsible to the people creates the expectation that government should meet the needs and correct the evils affecting particular groups in society. Confronted with the structural imperative of competitive elections every few years, political leaders can hardly do anything else.[46]

Neo-conservatives blame competitive electoral politics for

generating excessive expectations among the electorate. They also offer an additional reason: the political market differs from the economic in that, unlike the latter, it has no self-evident resource constraints. The connection between the services the citizens demand of the government and the costs of providing them remains extremely tenuous, and encourages fiscal irresponsibility in the electorate. Everyone wants the government to improve services, to do more, but expects someone else to pick up the cost. Clamour for higher benefits, better services and the like is unmatched by a willingness to pay higher taxes. The resulting deficit is but another expression of the overload. Electorates 'tend to expect too much from government action at too little cost' concludes Brittan.[47]

The erosion of 'traditional' restraints and values, claims the new Right, is yet another source of overload. In fact the idea that capitalist democracies have for a long time lived off their pre-modern legacy has been around in sociological circles (e.g. in Britain) for quite a while.[48] Brittan picks up this idea when he speaks of the 'vanishing heritage'. On the one hand, he suggests, such groups as the civil servants are no longer restrained by traditional notions of neutrality and disinterested service. On the other hand, workers and others (in short, the masses) are also no longer restrained by notions of hierarchy and deference. Indeed, given conditions of mass democracy the electorate seems to have accepted a form of self-restraint 'for a surprisingly long period'. But patriotism, the protestant work ethic, social deference, and the like, in short public morality of 'early capitalist bourgeois society', has proved to be transitional. It has largely been eroded, bringing organised self-interest into full play – whether in the private (industry) or public (government) sphere. Economic groups (read trade unions) are tending to exercise 'full market power' while electors are making 'excessive and incompatible' demands on government services.[49] While authority in general, and traditional sources of control in particular, have weakened there is no social consensus over principles of distribution or the processing of equity claims.

Paradoxically, increasing size and complexity of government is itself a part of the problem of overload. Once a system grows beyond a certain degree of complexity nobody can control its outcome.[50] Since governments reached this situation long ago (precisely when?), the result is a decline in government's effectiveness and control. This situation is described as 'public expenditure being out of control' or government itself being 'out of control'. In the optimistic post-war years it was believed that increased knowledge about social institutions would enable us to control and direct social phenomena intelligently. Social science was to provide us with this knowledge. But now men 'understand less and realise that they understand less' than they did 'twenty years ago'.[51] Then the world seemed familiar, and there was much more confidence in government's ability to achieve what it wanted. That confidence, according to King, has evaporated and the social world seems far less comprehensible.

It is, however, the American new Right that has made the failure of social knowledge its special *forte*. Thus Glazer speaks of the 'paradox of knowledge'. We know a good deal more about social policy than in the past yet at the same time we are 'becoming more uncertain about what measures will be most effective, if effective at all.'[52] The complexities and the ambiguities of the present contrast with the past when 'there was a clear field of action. The situation demanded that something be done; whatever was done was clear gain; little as yet was expected; little was known, and administrators approached their task with anticipation and self-confidence.'[53] Much of the social initiative of the 1960s, according to Moynihan, was based on the 'presumed knowledge' about the nature of social processes and social change. Following the success of Keynesian economic policies of the Kennedy administration, Moynihan's own hopes had been pinned on the social sciences to create a better society. He had thrown himself energetically into the making of social policy. By the end of the 1960s that social knowledge had turned out to be 'putative' rather than real, and Moynihan had lowered his sights a great deal: 'coping' was the best that social administrators and policy-makers could hope to achieve.[54]

This sense of disenchantment with scientific social engineering is quite widespread among American social scientists. But it is largely the new Right that has made it a major part of its argument against social planning and intervention. Analysts of other ideological persuasion, as we shall see, have drawn a different conclusion from the same situation. But for conservative thinkers the fundamental lesson of the experience of government action in the 1960s is to underline the fallacy inherent in the idea of social technology. Hayek, undoubtedly the most erudite exponent of this view, deplores the 'scientism' of social knowledge, the futility of aping the physical sciences in respect of knowledge and techniques of control. Human society, he points out, is not a product of deliberate design. Social institutions have not been planned, they have evolved over the centuries as a result of the spontaneous action and interaction of millions of people. The market is a good example:

We are only beginning to understand on how subtle a communications system the functioning of an advanced industrial society is based – a communications system which we call the market and which turns out to be a more efficient mechanism for digesting dispersed information than any that man has deliberately designed.[55]

Hayek, like all good conservatives, warns us not to tamper with social institutions, for we do not possess the knowledge that would enable us to shape society to our liking. This should teach 'the student of society a lesson in humility' and guard him against becoming an accomplice in 'men's fatal striving to control society'.[56]

Theorists such as Friedman and Hayek reject various forms of determinism – whether technological or sociological – which postulate the 'necessity' of big government. Criticising Galbraith, Friedman writes:

Large governments are not produced, and have not been produced, by technical necessities making things occur on a larger scale. There is no... necessity arising out of technological development that requires an expansion of welfare programmes, of rent controls, of government housing, of public health. Not one of these reflects technological pressure.[57]

Indeed, for the new Right, the market system and voluntary interaction more generally (the former is seen as the paradigm case of the latter) is far superior as a means of coordinating complex human activities and desires than state direction. No 'command' system, no bureaucratic method of planning could ever achieve, even with the help of coercion, what is achieved through the market. Indeed, according to neo-conservatives, the relationship between greater social complexity and state direction is the reverse of that postulated by sociological theories. Not only does increasing social complexity not require greater central direction and coordination, but rather complexity beyond a certain point makes it imperative that no single centre tries to comprehend, plan and execute courses of action.

As early as 1944 Hayek had argued that central planning and direction were more suited to 'comparatively simple conditions'.[58] Planning and effective control would not be difficult if 'conditions were so simple that a single person or board could effectively survey all the relevant facts. It is only as the factors which have to be taken into account become so numerous that it is impossible to gain a synoptic view of them, that decentralisation becomes imperative.'[59] The method of decentralised and voluntary (automatic) coordination of economic activity is far superior to the method of central direction which is 'incredibly clumsy, primitive, and limited in scope'. Under conscious central planning industry would never have reached 'the degree of differentiation, complexity, and flexibility it has attained.... Any further growth of complexity, therefore, far from making central direction more necessary, makes it more important than ever that we should use a technique that does not depend on conscious control.'[60]

Government growth, government failure and government overload thus form an interweaving set of arguments in favour of a minimal state. Increasing state intervention in the ordering of economic and social affairs is neither necessary nor beneficial. Government growth has been largely unprincipled, a product of expedient and shortsighted action on the part of sectional interests – politicians, voters, organised lobbies, bureaucracy and other vested interests – and has led to government overload. Much is promised by politicians and a great deal expected of governments: little is, and can be, delivered. The result is increasing frustration and confusion which ends in further government intervention and growth leading to yet more dissatisfaction. It is a vicious circle. King's rhetoric sums

41

it up nicely: 'Governments have tried to play God. They have failed. But they go on trying. How can they be made to stop?'[61] The solution is a return to sanity – to economic and social laisser-faire, to voluntarism and minimal state. Neo-conservatives are not opposed to a limited and modest form of social welfare, designed in such a way as to interfere least with the operation of market forces.[62] But anything going beyond that – and the post-war welfare state has gone far beyond that – is likely to be harmful for the economy. That is the lesson of the last thirty years and the key to understanding our current predicament.

The Welfare State and the Economic Crisis

The new Right is in no doubt about the source of current economic difficulties – it is the government, or more precisely the growth of government in the post-war years. Here Keynesianism emerges as the villain of the piece, and monetarism as the virtuous hero that will set things to right. The policies pursued by post-war governments, legitimised by Keynesian teachings, are largely to blame for the high rates of inflation in western economies.[63] First, Keynes taught that governments could maintain high levels of employment by injecting demand (money) into the system. But, as governments counter each recession by expanding credit and stimulating the economy, the money supply increases relative to the available goods and services. The result is inflation which tends to become cumulative. Second, and a related point, is that against the neo-classical view Keynes argued that a balanced budget was not essential for the health of market economies. In times of recession governments could run a deficit injecting demand into the system in order to expand output. Keynes, in short, sanctioned deficit financing as a way of stimulating the economy.[64]

Now as the neo-conservatives (in this case roughly monetarists) rightly point out, Keynes wanted the deficits to be balanced by budget surpluses in good years when demand was high and the economy buoyant. But – and this is the nub of the monetarist argument – in the post-war years what governments have practised is a form of irresponsible Keynes-ianism.[65] First, Keynesian remedies were meant for economic downturns rather more serious than those encountered in the 1950s and 1960s. But thanks to the spur of electoral popularity, stimulatory medicine was applied by the politicians with a free hand. Second, and more important, deficits were run in bad years, but not surpluses or even balanced budgets in good years. The reason for this is not hard to find. A surplus budget means either reduced public expenditure or higher taxation. But closing down government departments, winding up pro-grammes or raising taxes to create a budget surplus are not popular measures. They are not likely to win votes. Moreover, given the influence of the bureaucracy as well as pressures from other interests, retrenching government programmes and other activities are likely to prove difficult. In the 'political market' politicians compete for votes, and popular pressure is toward increased government programmes and reduced taxes. Politicians therefore take the easy way out and government expenditure tends to grow largely at the cost of deficits which involves either borrowing, printing money, or increasing the money supply in other ways to meet the growing needs of the state sector. The result is a steady push towards inflation.[66]

Attempts by governments to check inflation through in-comes and prices policies fail because, apart from their impracticability, they do not attack the problem at its roots. At best they provide a temporary respite after which inflation resumes its upward course. Control of the money supply, then, is the first major step necessary to curb inflation. But with this must go the determination by the government and the nation to 'live within its means'. This requires a balanced budget, bringing expenditure down to a level where it can be financed from revenue. That in turn means a reduction in the size of state activity. Rolling back the state – and in particular welfare activities of the state, for that is where expenditure has been growing fastest – becomes policy priority. In a sense, the project of the new Right is to undo the 'mischief' done to western economies by Keynesianism and liberal democracy during the last thirty years. It is a call to return to sound pre-war principles of finance like balanced budgets, and to the discipline of the market.[67]

43

Fuelling inflation is only one of the contributions of the post-war interventionist state to the difficulties of western capitalist economy. The so-called supply side economics, for instance, has focused on the effect of taxation and general government regulation of the economy on wealth creation.[68] The Keynesian doctrine of the management of demand assumed that government action will have no adverse effect on the supply side of capitalist economy. The dynamics of a capitalist economy, however, lies precisely in entrepreneurship, risk-taking, innovation and expectation of rewards. But excessive government regulation, high tax burdens and reduced profits all combine to stifle investment, growth and wealth creation. The modern state has become far too paternalistic and burdensome. If the economy is to be revitalised, the tax burden must be reduced, especially on those likely to be in the vanguard of economic advance, namely, managers, entrepreneurs and the rich. And if this looks like a plea for redistribution in favour of the rich, then 'supply siders' have a good argument for this. Reducing the tax burden of the rich, they say, will help the poor and the population at large. First, thanks to the new wealth created through these measures (the rich will invest rather than consume their income), the 'pie' will get bigger and everyone will be better off; second, at a more realistic (lower) rate of taxation the so-called 'black' economy will tend to decline – business transactions will be more open and tax avoidance and evasion will diminish. Thus the tax revenue will rise and so the burden of taxation on the middle and lower classes will be reduced.[69]

In sum, one set of arguments, largely associated with monetarist thinking, claims that in order to bring down inflation the money supply must be reduced. The other, largely associated with 'supply side' economics, claims that in order to stimulate economic recovery and promote growth business and industry must be 'deregulated', taxes reduced, private initiative encouraged and material incentives allowed full play. Both set of arguments converge on the notion that the state sector must be retrenched and the market forces, including voluntarism generally, allowed more free play. Not only welfare expenditure must be reduced, but also government attempt to maintain 'full employment' must be abandoned.

Unlike Keynesianism, the new Right sees unemployment as an unavoidable feature of market economies, a price to be paid for freedom and growth. If full employment is maintained 'artificially' – as all western countries have done to a greater or lesser extent – the result will be inflation, followed increasingly, as at present, by higher levels of unemployment. Moreover, government-induced full employment tends to distort the functioning of the market economy in harmful ways. Therefore a higher level of unemployment than what has been usual in post-war years may have to be regarded as 'natural'.[70]

But how can this programme of retrenching the welfare state be put into effect? Neo-conservatives believe that this is largely a question of mustering the political will necessary to carry out what are likely to be unpopular measures. But once public opinion is convinced of the rightness of the course then there is no reason why the programme of rolling back the state, reducing money supply and slshing taxes cannot be implemented. However, the new Right is aware that given the nature of the liberal political system the pressure on politicians, competing for popularity and votes, to expand government activity is very great. Some institutional safeguards are therefore necessary to keep in check politicians' propensity to overspend and make extragavant promises.

Neo-conservatives in the United States have suggested a variety of institutional devices. Among these are constitutional amendments such as an economic Bill of Rights which would limit the proportion of personal income deducted by government in taxes, save in exceptional circumstances. A variation on the same theme is a constitutional limitation on the proportion of national income that can be spent by the government.[71] Such institutional measures would restrict government spending and also ensure that social priorities are decided more carefully since choice will have to be exercised within strict budgetary constraints. Overall this is a novel and apparently serious proposal for insulating the market economy from the 'irrational' pressures stemming from liberal democratic politics. Note that it is not an attempt to depoliticise the economy completely, rather the aim is to limit the 'mischief' that democratic politics can do to the economy. Thus more than a law-and-order state is envisaged. For example, some social welfare activity is seen as a 'normal' feature of the modern capitalist state. What is considered objectionable and in need of control is the 'welfare drift' – the creeping collectivism and the incessant growth of government which is at once unnecessary, unprincipled and harmful.

So far such institutional checks on government growth have only been tried at the local or state level in the United States, and that too somewhat half-heartedly.[72] True, California's successful Proposition 13 – an anti-tax movement which led to a sharp cutback on property taxes – served to dramatise the idea of an institutional curb on government.[73] But, as though in answer to the new Right's prayer, conservative governments have been elected in both the UK and the USA pledged to implement the programme of the new Right through the normal political process. What have they achieved to date?

Neo-Conservatism in Action

The Thatcher government in Britain can claim the dubious honour of being the first western government returned on a platform of reducing taxes and curbing government spending. (It is important to note, however, that the latter was to be done chiefly through cutting out 'waste' and 'bureaucracy' and not by reducing services. Mrs Thatcher's victory at the polls was in no sense a repudiation of the welfare state by the electorate. See below pp. 84-7.) Although the pre-election policy statements of the Conservative Party were cautious and somewhat evasive, one thing was clear: under the leadership of Margaret Thatcher, Sir Keith Joseph and others, the Party had become converted to full-blooded monetarism, supply side economics and various other neo-conservatist beliefs – in short, to the political economy of the new Right.[74] The Thatcher administration came to power in May 1979. It was followed a year and a half later by the Reagan administration in the United States, which promised an even more dramatic turn towards the policies of the new Right. In so far as we can say of social doctrines 'By their fruit ye shall know them' these two experiments in neo-conservatism are of great interest, quite apart from their implications for human welfare. And, as examples of a new turn in policy, a decisive break with the post-war consensus over the welfare state, they deserve close attention.

The Thatcher government has had nearly four years in office (at the time of writing) to put its ideas into practice. What action has the government taken and what are its achievements to date? This is not the place to review the policies of the government and their outcome in detail. Rather our interest lies in the broader aspects of the question, especially from the viewpoint of the light it throws on the social doctrines of the new Right. Now, generally speaking, the neo-conservative strategy involves a two-pronged thrust. First, there is a monetarist approach to the economy in order to bring down inflation, involving a squeeze on the money supply through reduced government spending and borrowing, high interest rates, and the like. Second, while inflation is squeezed out of the system through a systematic reduction in the money supply, taxes are lowered in order to release initiative and provide incentives for investment and wealth-creation. Once the state is rolled back and public expenditure reduced, then government deficits can be brought down, taxes reduced further and eventually the budget balanced. This 'desocialisation' or 'destatification' of the economy enables the market forces to come into their own. The economy picks up and growth is resumed.[75]

So much for the scenario sketched by the new Right. Reality is quite another matter. When the Thatcher government took office it cut income taxes marginally, but simultaneously increased expenditure tax (VAT). Public expenditure could not be reduced overnight and if in the meanwhile government deficit was not to increase further then there was no alternative but increased taxation. Further reductions in income tax were promised but failed to materialise as the government found itself unable to reduce public expenditure.[76] Contrary to what was believed earlier, there was not a great deal of 'fat' (waste and inefficiency) in public services that could be so identified and eliminated. Worse still, government squeeze on the money supply (e.g. through high interest rates) led to bankruptcies and a steep rise in unemployment. While the expected economic miracle failed to appear and the economy went from bad to worse, rising unemployment began to make heavy demands on the public purse. At the time of writing unemployment has soared above 3 million or well over 10 per cent of the labour force. True, inflation has been brought down, but at a heavy price paid in business bankruptcies and unemployment.[77]

Well before Mrs Thatcher came to power, social welfare expenditure had been reduced by the Labour government in the face of worldwide recession and mounting budget deficits.[78] The Thatcher government may thus be seen as having continued, rather than accelerated, this trend. In other words, the cuts instituted by the government have not been as deep as feared initially though clearly virtually all services – except defence and law and order – are starved of funds.[79] To some extent, government's inability to reduce public expenditure and cut back social services stems from the fact that within the framework of a liberal democracy – government by consent, influence of organised interest groups, the rule of law, the principle of honouring past commitments – change, whether towards the Left or the Right, is necessarily slow and piecemeal. Short of draconian measures, which would probably have to include the suspension of elections and the introduction of authoritarian government, new policies cannot be implemented in a drastic way. Moreover, Britain's public service workers, professionals and others, are well organised and able to offer stiffer opposition to cutbacks, than say, workers in the United States.[80] Lastly, three decades of the welfare state has created a social climate – a diffuse framework of values – in which drastic reduction in the services and large-scale redundancies in the public sector could strain the social order to the utmost.

In sum, the norms and institutions of a liberal democracy, the strength of organised interest groups and, more indirectly, the prospect of electoral competition all act as a counterweight to radical change. The new Right accused Keynes of failing to take into account the sociopolitical context in which his policies had to work. Ironically, the new Right itself seems not to have appreciated the political constraints within which its own bitter remedies have to be applied. Political constraints have undoubtedly limited the full-blooded implementation of Thatcherite economic and social policies. But overall what is remarkable about the four years of Thatcherism is the extent to which policies of the new Right, which represent a sharp break with post-war consensus, have been unflinchingly applied. What these years also show, by and large, is the failure of monetarism and supply side economics to lift the economy out of stagnation. What seems to be taking place in Britain is better described as a government-induced recession ('piggy-backed' on a world recession), through deflationary policies, resulting in massive unemployment. On the debit side of the balance the record looks extraordinarily 'good', on the credit side – the stimulus to economic investment and growth – it looks equally 'bad', so far. Even the leading employers' association which supported the government policy initially, later became wary of rigid monetarism urging goverment to follow an expansionary course.[81] As far as the social services are concerned, what we are witnessing is an attempt to halt and roll back state welfare indirectly, largely through a policy of attrition. While public services have been put on belt-tightening exercise, privatisation is being encouraged by the government and appears to be making good progress in some areas.[82]

In the United States the situation is very different. Compared with Britain, and Western Europe more generally, the American welfare state has a weaker base of support and legitimacy. The current of neo-conservative thinking on welfare runs deeper. The counterweight of a political party based on a relatively coherent philosophy of welfare and social spending, such as the socialist parties of Europe, is absent. Trade union membership is a good deal lower than in Europe and the influence of labour much weaker generally.[83] There are also constitutional differences. For example, unlike the prime minister in the British Cabinet system, the American president is not hamstrung by a ministerial collective.

It is not therefore surprising that within a much shorter term in office President Reagan has cut both social programmes and taxes (especially the latter) substantially. Despite a large and mounting government deficit, the administration has stuck to its policy of tax cuts believing that 'supply side' effects would begin to pull the economy out of recession and provide the basis for a market-based recovery. Further cuts in public spending are scheduled for the coming years. The President has also announced a policy of New Federalism under which many social programmes at present run by the federal government are to be handed over (returned in many cases) to the state and local jurisdictions. This is part of a package of reducing 'big government' and, in effect, federal responsibility for many areas of welfare.[84] Not untypically for the United States, social spending as well as taxes have been slashed by the President with great gusto. As Alvin Schorr writes, the social services appear to 'have been cut faster and deeper in America than in Britain'. Indeed, Schorr suggests that benefit levels have suffered absolute reductions in the United States and if inflation is taken into account the American personal social services would have been 'nearly halved' within a year or two.[85] Yet the cuts, which have hurt the poor most, have evoked little overt social protest. Part of the reason seems to be that the American population is least supportive of that aspect of welfare – public assistance-type programmes for the poor – which has borne the brunt of the cuts.[86] Nonetheless the Republicans have suffered losses in the mid-term congressional elections which points to the electorate's concern over cuts in social programmes and rising unemployment. A tight monetary policy appears to have helped bring down inflation substantially, but interest rates remain high (1982) fuelling unemployment. Meanwhile, there are some signs of recovery but it is too early to say if the American economy is at last coming out of recession.[87]

If the poor in America are quiescent, the rich are not altogether approving of the cuts. At a recent meeting of top business executives in New York the President of the Time Inc. voiced his disquiet at the fact that the cuts were falling largely on the poor and the elderly. This, he thought, may be counter-productive, and could have an adverse effect on the recent groundswell in America in favour of free enterprise and capitalism (incidentally a good example of the relevance of social policy for the legitimisation of the social system of capitalism).[88] In fact, right-wing rhetoric notwithstanding, opinion polls show that neither the majority of the British nor American population is in favour of cuts in major social services such as education, health care and income maintenance. It is only in respect of 'welfare' (means-tested assistance to the poor) that a very substantial minority favours reduced spending. True, the electorate would also like to see lower taxes and less government bureaucracy (less waste and unnecessary expenditure[89]), but service workers, such as teachers, doctors, nurses and social workers are not 'bureaucracy'; nor are transfer payments, e.g. pensions. Yet cash transfers and reimbursements, the salaries of profesionals and para-professionals, and various essential commodities form the bulk of social expenditure in all western countries.[90]

Clearly, the electorate is not against social welfare services. Even in the United States there is no evidence that the majority of Americans are fed up with the welfare state and want social programmes cut. It is not inconsistent to favour lower taxes and a reduction in government spending generally and at the same time support health, education, job training, affirmative action and similar government programmes.[91] In this sense there is no tax-welfare backlash in the United States. Dissatisfaction with the increasing burden of taxation in a stagnant economy, and in particular the success of Proposition 13 in California, was seen by neo-conservatives as the signal of a general tax revolt against the Big State. It was expected that such movements would spread to the rest of the United States and other western countries. But subsequent years have not borne out these expectations. 'Tax revolts' such as Proposition 13 must therefore be seen in proper perspective. Wilensky's careful study of the United States and other industrial nations shows that tax protests of this kind are best seen as a reaction against the rapid rise in a highly visible, regressive and unpopular tax, namely a tax on property.[92]

Be that as it may, both the Thatcher and Reagan administrations came to power with the general policy of retrenching big government and cutting taxes. Bringing down inflation, reducing and eventually eliminating budget deficit and setting the economy on the growth path once again were some of the prime objectives. The neo-conservative strategy has had more time to work in Britain than in the United States, at the time of writing. The results of the Thatcher experiment seem dubious to say the least. Budget deficits have not been rising, but the prospect of a balanced budget remains as remote as ever. Perhaps a massive increase in unemployment is the most visible result. However the unions and the workers generally have been cowed into moderating wage demands while productivity in industry is said to have risen appreciably. Inflation has been slowing down, but so far there has been no sharp rise in investment nor signs of much new enterprise turning the emaciated British economy into a state of robust health. Will 'Reaganomics' prove to be very different? It seems unlikely. The Reagan administration launched its policy with an emphasis on the 'supply side', that is with substantial tax cuts. At the same time a tight monetary policy together with other recessionary factors has reduced inflation substantially. But interest rates are still high, unemployment has been rising and, because of the tax cuts, there is a budget deficit of gigantic proportions. In short, there is no sign of the 'magic' of supply side economics beginning to work.[93]

A further question that must be asked is how would the electorate respond to what eventually must appear as a failure of these regimes to deliver? The irony of this situation is that government failure would seem to apply to conservative governments as much as to the others. Moreover, as one observer of the American scene suggests Ronald Reagan's (and by implication Margaret Thatcher's) promises to the electorate may themselves, in retrospect, turn out to be a kind of inflated politics – the politics of 'vote motive'.[94] What drove the populace into the arms of the new Right was largely the failure of the mixed economy – the child of Keynesianism – to overcome stagflation and its attendant evils. Since various old remedies had been tried but were no longer working the electorate was ready to give something different, and new in the context of post-war consensus, a chance. In the short run, the new policies have succeeded in redistributing incomes in favour of the rich, increasing unemployment, reducing social services and, at least in the United States, reducing the living standards of the poor palpably.[95] True, inflation has come down but the hoped-for economic recovery looks as distant as ever (but see p. 50 above for the United States). It could of course be argued, as politicians such as Thatcher do, that the new policies need more time to work than the life-span of a single government. Ideologues of the Right echo this claim in suggesting that a much longer time-span is needed to undo the harm done by the policies pursued over the last thirty years. (This sounds rather like a 'transition to capitalism' in the manner of the long drawn out 'transition to communism'). Indeed helped, in part, by the Falklands war and a Labour Party much weakened through internal dissension the Conservatives have succeeded in winning another term of office. This should provide neo-conservatism with all the time needed to move Britain further to the Right. The re-election of Reagan in 1984 could do the same for the United States.

The New Right and Social Welfare: An Evaluation

Neo-conservatism pre-dates the economic crisis of the 1970s. But it is the conundrum of stagflation – which has confounded Keynesian wisdom – that has provided market theorists and many disenchanted liberals (especially in America) with the opportunity to revive and refurbish the doctrines of *laisser-faire*. Although many of the arguments advanced have been developed in the light of the post-war experience of the welfare state there is little in the social doctrine of the new Right that cannot be found in the writings of classical *laisser-faire* thinkers such as Herbert Spencer. The economic arguments also represent essentially a return to pre-Keynesian, neo-classical thinking. Moreover a mere glance at the writings of the new Right will show that what we have to contend with is essentially an ideology rather than a 'scientific' theory amenable to a 'test' of falsification or verification – albeit this is true, to a greater or lesser extent, of all social doctrines. In any case, it is necessary to take the arguments advanced seriously – they already form the intellectual support for the new policy initiatives in the UK and the USA – and also to attempt an evaluation. To this we now turn.

Space does not permit an elaborate critique of neo-conservatism. The main themes can be summarised as follows:

1 A tendency to exaggerate and generalise on the basis of insufficient evidence.
2 The use of highly selective evidence.
3 A one-sided and biased view of government functioning.

4 An inadequate conception of the role of democracy and politics in modern societies.
5 A failure to recognise the problem of *social* integration in a market society, namely how to counter the socially disruptive effects of the market economy and maintain a cohesion of the *national* community.

Let us examine these in turn.

Whilst there is a grain of truth in many of the neo-conservative arguments, it tends to be magnified out of all proportion. It is one thing to claim, for instance, that vested interests – politicians competing for votes, bureaucracies and professionals concerned with enhancing their own position – have contributed to the growth of the post-war welfare state. But it is quite another to suggest, as neo-conservatives seem to do, that much or most of the growth in welfare expenditure can be attributed to these sources. Studies conducted by the OECD, for example, have shown that a good deal of the growth in welfare expenditue can be accounted for by such 'automatic' factors as an ageing population, relative price effect, maturity of pension programmes, and the like.[96] Much is made by the new Right of the bureaucracy's role in expanding state activities, but little is offered by way of hard evidence which might allow the nature and extent of this influence to be assessed. Again, the 'vote motive' theory of welfare plays down the role of ideological differences among political parties and also fails to appreciate the nature of post-war consensus over welfare which formed part of a wider climate of 'social' concern. Witness, for example, the burgeoning of private pension schemes and other employee benefits.

Exaggeration can also be seen in the idea that the social policies of the 1960s were largely based on the promise of the social sciences. Neo-conservatives play down or ignore the fact, well researched and well known to every policy analyst, that policy-making is a 'political' process and that government rhetoric about social science cannot be taken at its face value. Thus to claim that social policy has 'failed' and, by implication, should be abandoned because social science is unable to provide authentic knowledge is at best to take a naive view of policy-making and at worst to misrepresent the nature of the policy-making process grossly. It is to start, quite wrongly, by depoliticising the process in the first place and then castigating it because it does not measure up to 'scientific' expectations.

Budget deficits provide yet another example of exaggeration and sweeping generalisation. First, neo-conservatives present the 'deficit' in government account as something quite self-evident and 'objective'. This is misleading since government deficit is hardly an unproblematic notion.[97] Secondly, neo-conservatives fail to point out that it is only in the 1970s, largely because of the recession, that sizeable deficits have begun to emerge.[98] On the whole, economists believe that until the late 1960s government revenue and expenditure were roughly in balance in most western countries.[99] But the new Right often conveys the impression that, under the influence of Keynesianism, western governments have been running budget deficits throughout the post-war years. Perhaps it should also be pointed out that the new Right pays scant attention to the budgetary and inflationary consequences of the wars, for example the Korean war, and more particularly, the Vietnam war.

Neo-conservative arguments differ in their level of abstraction and theoretical sophistication. But on the whole they tend to be one-sided and rely on highly selective evidence. For instance, much is made of the growing scale and complexity of government. Systems, it is claimed, get 'out of control' beyond a certain level of complexity. The new Right uses this argument to criticise government growth and centralisation (see pp. 38, 41 above). Yet what it fails to note is that alongside the modern government, giant corporations have arisen whose operations are worldwide and whose organisational complexities match, if not exceed, those of the government. (The latter, for example, is a 'national' undertaking and in this sense of somewhat limited scope and complexity.) Few theorists of 'overload' take cognizance of the fact that the highly complex, centralised, worldwide empires of the multinationals are apparently quite successful and well under control. Moreover, the obvious point that 'big' government may not be an aberration in a world of big corporations, big unions and professional associations seems to have escaped them.

Neo-conservative literature abounds in examples of the use of highly selective evidence. Friedman, for example, looks at two countries that have run into increasing difficulty in recent years: Britain and Sweden. He blames the welfare state, by implication, for Britain's economic ills – poor growth, inflation, unemployment and the like. Sweden, Friedman concedes, has 'done far better than Britain'. But he has a ready explanation for this. It was 'spared the burden of two world wars and, indeed, reaped economic benefits from its neutrality.'[100] With a sleight of hand Britain's misfortunes are laid at the door of welfare while Sweden's good fortune is ascribed to something else, something which presumably overcame all the 'evil' consequences of big government. Again Friedman stresses recent dissatisfaction in Sweden, but fails to mention the fact that this European Welfare State with all its 'bureaucracy', 'waste', disincentive to work and save, evil effect on the family, and the like has maintained a decent rate of growth during the post-war years, had a very low rate of unemployment throughout the 1970s and enjoys a per capita income surpassing that of the United States.[101] Other European countries (e.g. West Germany and Austria), which have managed to combine high levels of social expenditure and social protection with excellent economic growth as well as low rates of inflation and unemployment (relatively speaking, of course) in recent years are hardy mentioned. Clearly, to dub these cases as government failure would be to stretch credulity too far. They are therefore simply ignored.

In any case since in the English-speaking world Britain symbolised the aspirations and achievements of the post-war welfare state it becomes the whipping-boy of neo-conservatives. Thus Kristol writes that Britain is becoming poorer 'with every passing year' because of a 'massive redistribution of income, through high rates of taxation.[102] Quite apart from the fanciful notion of a 'massive' income redistribution in Britain, Kristol chooses to ignore countries such as Sweden and Austria which have become successively richer despite (because of?) high rates of taxation. Moreover, the neo-conservative argument (or more often insinuation) that social expenditure and high taxation is responsible for Britain's poor post-war economic growth ignores two important points. First, Britain has had a low rate of economic growth from the mid-nineteenth century to the second world war. In other words, the low growth rate pre-dates the advent of the welfare state. Second, Britain's growth rate in the 1950s and 1960s – the years of social welfare and high taxation – had in fact been close to an all-time high.[103] No doubt it would be argued that but for the welfare state Britain would have done even better. And, writing in the 1980s, we would be guilty of intellectual bad faith if we were to deny that social science cannot provide reliable, definitive answers to such questions. In social (i.e. including economic and political) arguments it is not long before we find ourselves in the realm of sheer ideology, making assertions and counter-assertions which can in no way be validated either by a compelling general theory or by incontrovertible evidence. But this behoves us to be cautious and somewhat less assured of our knowledge. Yet neo-conservatives, notably Friedman and Kristol, seem hardly troubled by such problems. They *know* – and know that they know.

The biased and one-sided nature of the neo-conservative argument can be seen clearly in the notion of government failure. This completely ignores the fact that the goverment is not an undertaking of the same kind as, say, a business seeking profit, or a football team trying to win a championship. The government, in many ways, must be seen as a part of the 'polity' which is an arena for the articulation and contestation of interests (material and well as ideational). By definition, a democratic government cannot but act through politics. Its 'rationality' consists in being a vehicle for certain values (e.g. responsiveness to citizen interests, governing through consent rather than fiat, etc.) To a large extent, therefore, government tends to have an 'expressive' rather than an 'instrumental' orientation. Hence what appears as government 'failure', for example in weakened authority resulting from greater demo-cracy and participation, may precisely be its 'success'. But the new Right tends to see the government largely in 'instrumental' terms, in the manner of a business undertaking or a military operation whose criteria of success are fairly precise and self-evident. Thus King inveighs against the British government for its 'failure' to achieve an incomes policy.[104] But to think in terms of a simple dichotomy – success/failure, good/bad – in relation to government action, and especially in such a highly contentious area as incomes policy, is to oversimplify grossly. Secondly, to condemn 'government' as such on the basis of the *British* government's failure in incomes policy is to generalise on the basis of somewhat limited and one-sided evidence. If King had taken the trouble to look at some other European countries, Austria, for example, he would have found some very 'successful' governments.

More generally, neo-conservatives choose to play down what might be considered government 'successes' while dwelling at length on 'failures'. Thus King provides a lengthy catalogue of failures but only makes a passing reference to post-war full employment which at least he acknowledges as a government success (at a more modest level King could have mentioned the Open University).[105] In the United States, social scientists of the new Right, as well as of other persuasions, see the welfare reforms of the Johnson era as a failure. Yet a more careful and systematic appraisal of that experience by neo-conservatives themselves shows that there was much in the War on Poverty and Great Society programmes that could be seen as government success.[106] Indeed, at one point, Wildavsky, for example, concedes that government action aimed at the redistribution of resources, or the organisation of specific services such as health care, appears to succeed quite well. It fails where it tries to modify human behaviour – changing the attitudes and practices of the poor, for example.[107] Yet this critical distinction between forms of government action that succeed and others that do not has received scant attention in the vast American literature on the failure of social policy.

More important, the largely technicist conception of social policy held by the vast majority of social scientists in the United States almost guarantees the 'failure' of social policy. For if the latter is seen in terms of clearly formulated objectives and the appropriate means to achieve them (with social science providing the link), then given the 'political' and 'dialectical' nature of the policy process the outcome is bound to appear 'messy' and quite other than that envisaged in the blueprint. To label this discrepancy between the ideal and the actual as failure is to take a naive view of policy. It is to take the metaphor of 'social engineering' literally. In contrasting two differing notions of policy a perceptive American social scientist, Horowitz, goes to the heart of the matter. 'The British concept of policy is clearly political.'[108] The social science input in Britain, he suggests, is far more effective in policy terms 'because of its frank espousal of political party platforms and partisan considerations'. In the United States, on the other hand, policy is seen in terms of expertise, as a part of the executive branch of the government. This assumes a 'universalism which is more apparent than real.'[109]

Webber, an American urban planner, puts it even more plainly. He shares the mood of disappointed hopes of the programmes of the 1960s with neo-conservatives but offers an entirely different diagnosis of the problem. He sees the issue, quite rightly in my view, as over-reliance on 'professional' and 'neutral' techniques of problem solving. In other words, what neo-conservatives see as government failure and the failure of the idea of social policy itself Webber sees as the failure of the 'technicist' view of policy-making. Wherever 'alternative programmes with divergent institutional outcomes are possible, there can be no one right way . . . there are no scientifical or technically correct answers, only politically appropriate ones.'[110] He now thinks of policy planning 'as a subset of politics, its central function being to improve the processes of public debate and public decision.'[111] I agree with Webber entirely. Complaints about government failure and policy failure may therefore be seen more appropriately as the failure of an apolitical, consensual and scientistic model of policy.

The same mechanistic model of social action seems to lie behind the new Right's litany of complaints about 'unintended consequences' of government action. Here the underlying assumption is that of 'social engineering' – a linear, one-to-one relationship between variables. This fails to appreciate that the social system involves a complex web of cause-and-effect relationships which make for a 'dialectical' process of development and change. Wildavsky's grouse that 'solutions become problems faster than we can cope'[112] should be seen more as an insight, for it amounts to discovering that social development is a *dialectical* process where there are no neat, final solutions. What neo-conservatives are indirectly complaining about is that the model of scientific knowledge, and the plan of action based on it, is quite inappropriate in the social field, an idea that has been implicit in, for example, Titmuss's approach to social policy since the early post-war years.[113] In short, this approach suggests that we cannot really take 'politics' out of 'policy'. Nor can we find 'final' solutions to social problems. Turning the coin over, so to speak, we could say that social intervention can never be simply a matter of 'intelligence' or 'technique'.

This leads us to the inadequate notion of politics and its role in modern society which seems to underlie much of neo-conservative thinking. Clearly, economists such as Friedman and Hayek would like to see the capitalist market economy depoliticised as much as possible. Both are in favour of constitutional restrictions on the extent to which the political order may be allowed to interfere with and modify the 'spontaneous' order of the market. For Hayek the 'fatal defect' of liberal democracies is the unlimited power granted to elected assemblies which leaves them open to 'blackmail' by all sorts of organised groups. He speaks of the 'enormous and exceedingly wasteful apparatus of para-government' that has grown up 'consisting of trade associations, trade unions and professional organisations, designed primarily to divert as much as possible of the stream of governmental favour to their members.'[114] This 'unlimited democracy' can only be restricted by 'limiting the powers of government'.[115]

This is a far cry from the idea of the modern state as an association of the community with a democratically elected government ruling through consent, bearing overall responsibility for the nation's well-being and therefore necessarily exercising control and regulation over many areas of social life. These developments, spread over the last hundred years or so, have formed an integral part of the growth of the modern nation-state and citizenship. What we have witnessed from about the last quarter of the nineteenth century is the politicisation of society from below, the gradual admission of the masses to the exercise of political rights. This democratic revolution has been part and parcel of the evolution of the liberal market society. Clearly neo-conservatism would like to reverse this process by curtailing the democratic element in that somewhat contradictory combination 'liberal democracy'.

Whether such a reversal is feasible or not is not the issue here. The important point to note is that the critique of democratic politics by the new Right shows, indirectly, the conflict between the basic principles underlying the market economy and those underlying democracy. Far from being the ideal 'political shell' of a capitalist economy – as vulgar Marxism claims[116] – the democratic principle and interest group politics introduce an important contradiction within the social system of western capitalism. The new Right, which sees society as really the market writ large, recognises this contradiction and would resolve it by curtailing democracy and largely depoliticising the economy. Clearly, for neo-conservatives, the modern polity itself, rather like the modern welfare state, is a kind of 'unprincipled' growth, an incubus on the liberal market order which the latter could do without. Such, at any rate, seems to be the concept of politics underlying much of neo-conservative thinking today.

The final point is related to the one just sketched above. The neo-conservative argument is premised on the values of individualism, liberty and property rights, and on inequality as the natural outcome of the workings of the market.[117] Focused on atomised individuals it has no conception of the nation-state as a community nor any idea of the *social* (as distinct from *individual*) consequences of the market order that may need political intervention. The inadequacy of unbridled individualism in coming to terms with the problem of social solidarity was the principal critique levelled by Durkheim against Spencerian anti-collectivism.[118] The problem has remained essentially unchanged. The growth of nationalism and imperialism at the turn of the century seems to have compelled liberalism, in Britain, to abandon the dogma of social *laisser-faire* and to embark on extensive social legislation. Later the disastrous social and political consequences of mass unemployment in the 1930s led to the development of the New Deal in the US and – via the second world war – to the comprehensive welfare state. Wars, as Titmuss and others have demonstrated, have played an important part in the elaboration and application of social principles which recognised something higher than the market order: the national *community*.[119] The logic of radical anti-collectivism (e.g.

Hayek) is to demand that 'free man' puts up with the 'costs' of a market order if he wants its benefits. But in the real social world – as distinct from the philosopher's study or model of society – we not only have rational individuals playing the game of 'catallaxy'[120] but also such beings as workers, Jews, Fascists, communists and such things as guns, tanks, bombs and concentration camps. Perhaps Professor Hayek's 'spontaneous order' includes the Nazi movement and the second world war, but I am sure even he would not wish humanity to pay so dearly for 'spontaneity', especially as it could also spell the end of the market order once and for all.

The same atomistic individualism prevents the new Right from recognising the problem of 'social justice'. If society is seen as consisting simply of individuals playing the game of the market according to the current rules and taking their chances in the market-place, for better or worse, then where is the problem of 'social' justice? It disappears. First, because there is nothing called 'social' where there are only individuals. Second, in a market order which has evolved over the years spontaneously and whose consequences are unplanned and unintended (e.g. the mass unemployment of the 1930s) *who* is being unjust? No one. There are no evil motives at work – no malevolent will of a dictator or a government apart from what the market order 'blindly' decrees – to be held 'responsible' for any individual's fate. The market order, like nature itself, knows neither justice nor injustice.[121] True, the logic of this argument cannot be faulted, but the point is that it makes for a highly unrealistic (and counter-intuitive) view of the social order. The idea of a 'just' social order – fairness as a property of social arrangements – is a fundamental notion of social philosophy based on human experience. It cannot therefore be dismissed so lightly.[122] Second, the fatalism implied in the view that submission to the 'spontaneous' market order is the best we can do – whatever it may bring in its wake – is at odds with the entire western spirit of activism and mastery of the environment.

The main problem is that the new Right is profoundly asocial and ahistorical in its thinking. It takes no cognizance of the disruptive *social* consequences of a spontaneous economic order. The problem of social conflict over distributive and life-chance issues generally does not seem to concern anti-collectivists. Their ahistorical approach (or, if it is preferred, mistaken view of history) looks at the market order in an 'ideal' sense, abstracted from history. The actual history of market capitalism is inseparable from colonialism and imperialism, from class conflicts of Titanic proportions, and from national wars. The idea that the market order has evolved spontaneously also involves a gross misrepresentation.[123] History rather shows a mixture of spontaneity and intervention by the political authority. Does Henry VIII's dissolution of the monasteries and break with Rome form a part of spontaneous development? And what of the enclosure movement in England? And the repeal of various neo-mercantilist legislation, including the Corn Laws? Are they a part of spontaneity even though they involved state intervention? Indeed without these forms of state involvement it is difficult to see how the market system, private property and free wage labour could have made their appearance. A great deal of violence and coercion were involved in these changes.

To sum up: the absence of any conception of the nation-state as a community, the denial of the social, the attempt to constitute a rather spurious 'spontaneously' evolving market order and endow it with a sense of sacred fatality, the absence of any historical appreciation of capitalist development makes neo-conservatism highly inadequate both intellectually and as a viable practical doctrine for advanced industrial democracies.

Let us conclude, however, on a positive note by pointing out what seems worthwhile in the neo-conservative approach. Friedman writes:

the nineteenth-century experience highlighted the advantages of the invisible hand [a reference to Adam Smith] – and also the economic, social, and political problems to which it gave rise. The twentieth-century experience has highlighted the advantages of the paternal state – and also the economic, social, and political problems to which it gave rise.[126]

This is neatly put. It is precisely this other side of the dialectic of welfare, with which we are confronted at the moment, that the critique of the new Right has highlighted. From an intellectual and moral standpoint we may reject the Right's approach to the current crisis. Moreover, in terms of its own value parameters and expectations the practical results of its policies have been, to put it mildly, disappointing. All the same, the new Right has articulated an all-embracing critique of the welfare state. This is a challenge to which those who believe the welfare state to be an institution both viable and worth defending must respond. The idea of a 'political market', the problem of unintended condequences of action in respect of government growth and government failure, the economic consequences of social policy, the critique of functionalist (deterministic) theories of the state, the problem of efficiency in the public sector are all important questions related to the post-war development of the welfare state. The grossly exaggerated claims and one-sided arguments concerning these points must be rejected. But, that said, it cannot be denied that the critique raises issues which, in the complacency bred by the long success of the mixed economy ('the golden age of the welfare state', as Gough puts it[125]), have largely been ignored. It is important to confront these if we believe, as I do, that some form of a mixed system in which the state remains responsible for general welfare provides the best path of development for western liberal societies.

3 The Marxist Alternative: the not so new Left

Marxism is perhaps the most fascinating intellectual and political adventure of our times. At once revolutionary politics, secular religion, utopian fantasy, social theory, hard-headed analysis of capitalism, philosophy of history, scientific socialism, and much else besides, it has continued to haunt capitalism for over a century. Many a time have its 'bourgeois' opponents been convinced that the theory has at last been laid to rest in the graveyard of the history of ideas. Each time it has come back from the dead to mock 'bourgeois' social science and to challenge its hollow pretensions. The fortunes of Marxism have waxed as the fortunes of capitalism have waned. Little wonder then that in the 1970s, as capitalist economy has got into deep trouble, the shadow of Marxism has once again begun to loom large.

The post-war years found Marxism in retreat. Thanks, in part, to state intervention in general and to the management of demand in particular what the western nations experienced was not a slide back into recession but a magnificent economic boom unprecedented in their history. Not only was employment maintained at a high level – far beyond the hopes of even the most optimistic Keynesians – but the standard of living rose rapidly giving currency to extravagant notions of 'post-capitalism', the 'affluent society', and the 'end of ideology'. At any rate, post-war developments were so much out of line with the prognostications of Marxist theory – the impending collapse of capitalism and the immiseration of the working classes – that Marxist 'science' found itself in disarray. In many ways the inter-war years had confirmed the Marxist scenario. The contradictions inherent in capitalism, notably between the forces and the relations of production, had brought the system on the verge of collapse and had resulted in intense conflict between capital and labour. Many Marxists believed that the end of capitalism was at hand and that the socialist society predicted by Marx would soon rise out of the ruins of capitalism. In the event, not only was there no proletarian revolution in any advanced capitalist country but after the war capitalism rose like a phoenix from its ashes dazzling its friends and foes alike by its dynamism and vitality.

As the expected economic downturn and the resulting crisis of capitalism failed to materialise Marxists found increasing difficulty in making sense of the post-war western world. The gap separating Marxist theory from contemporary reality was so great as to undermine the former's credibility seriously. Writing in the early 1960s a Marxist economist noted that in western academic circles Marxist theory 'meets only with indifference or contempt'.[1] This, he believed, could not be explained by such crude notions as academic science being in the pay of the bourgeoisie. The reasons were largely intellectual. Marxist writers had been 'content to repeat Marx's teachings ... which have increasingly lost contact with contemporary reality.[2] In a similar vein, Baran and Sweezy, veteran American Marxists, bemoaned the meagre contribution made by Marxists to the understanding of post-war western society. Content to 'repeat familiar formulations' they had been confounded by the fact that two decades had passed 'since the end of the second world war without the recurrence of severe depression'.[3] These judgements may be somewhat harsh, but they draw attention to two things. First, that post-war western society was not easy to grasp in terms of pre-war Marxist thinking, and second, that the development of western Marxism was stultified by the Stalinist and Soviet hegemony.

Be that as it may, the comments of Mandel, and Baran and Sweezy, concerned primarily with economic analysis, are applicable a fortiori to the analysis of political and social aspects of capitalism. For the emphasis in Marxist theory is on the mode of production – the way productive activities are structured and the power relationships that flow from it – as the central fact about society. It is this economic structure or the 'material' base that determines the nature of the political, social and ideological processes (the superstructure) of society.

Given the centrality of economics, classical Marxist theory paid little attention to the analysis of political and social institutions. The latter tended to be seen largely as derived and thus second order phenomena – a 'reflection' of the economic order. Now one of the key characteristics of post-war capitalism has been the enhanced role of the state, especially in the form of the welfare state. Yet as far as understanding the state and its relationship with the capitalist economy was concerned the theoretical legacy of classical Marxism was meagre. It was not until the late 1960s that a systematic Marxist analysis of the state began.[4] By the mid-1970s there was a spate of Marxist writings on social theory, including the analysis of the state. Although a good deal of this debate remains highly formal and abstract Marxist theory has made impressive advances in 'incorporating' the capitalist state within its basic explanatory schema.[5] The 'welfare state' naturally features as one aspect of the activity of the capitalist state.

For the best part of the 1960s and early 1970s, Marxist analyses of the welfare state (few and far between in any case and often a part of some larger critique of capitalism) were largely concerned with debunking the social democratic view of welfare. For example, Marxists pointed out that far from being an embryonic form of socialism, brought into being by social democratic governments, the social services were to be found in all advanced capitalist societies. These services were largely a 'necessity' for capitalism. On the one hand they helped to make capitalism more efficient and productive, and on the other hand they acted as a form of social control mechanism, helping to maintain social peace and to legitimise capitalism. Marxists, with other radicals, argued strongly that the welfare state had not altered the class structure of capitalism in any significant way. Contrary to popular belief, fostered by social democracy, the welfare state did not redistribute income from the rich to the poor. It was a form of horizontal distribution involving intra-class transfer of resources. In short, the welfare state was no socialist measure.[6]

What Marxist analysis did mainly was to provide a systematic, theoretical explanation for the observed facts of welfare in this respect. The facts themselves had been researched by social democratic scholars such as Titmuss and

Townsend. But whereas they were content to offer *ad hoc* explanations for the limited achievements of social welfare, and exhorted public opinion to support more egalitarian social policies (assuming that *moral* suasion would help to bring about change), Marxists offered *structural* explanations of the limits of state welfare. Arguing that the state was, in the last analysis, a creature of the mode of production concerned with maintaining and reproducing its essential features, the requirements of the economic system itself placed definite limits on the nature and scope of social reform. In short, the structure of the capitalist system itself explained the limits of social policy.[7]

It must also be kept in mind that when Marxist social science revived in the late 1960s it found itself in an intellectual environment dominated by functionalist sociology, systems theory, structuralism and other 'synchronic' analyses of society. In particular, the influential school of Althusserian Marxism took a highly 'structural-functionalist' view of society.[8] At a level of empirical reality, too, capitalist society looked very well-integrated. Full employment, steady economic growth, a low rate of inflation, increasing social expenditure, such were the characteristics of western capitalism. Theory as well as material conditions encouraged a form of radical functionalism, expressed in the tendency to explain how a particular 'part' or institution in capitalist society worked for the benefit of the 'whole'. This approach was especially evident in respect of the welfare state.[9] However, as welfare capitalism began to show signs of malaise in the 1970s, Marxist analysis began to show a greater awareness of the dysfunctions of state intervention for the capitalist economy. 'Crisis' began to appear more frequently in Marxist vocabulary and more recent writings on the welfare state have taken up the themes of 'contradiction' and 'crisis' in advanced capitalism.[10] This is not to suggest either that such themes were totally absent from earlier writings or that Marxist analysis of welfare has now ceased to be 'functionalist'. The point is that Marxism is a comprehensive enough theory to include functions as well as dysfunctions, integration as well as conflict and as the material reality of capitalism has changed so the emphasis in Marxist analysis has shifted towards contradictions and conflicts of welfare capitalism.

The Crisis of Welfare Capitalism

Not unlike the neo-conservatives, Marxists too find post-war welfare capitalism a contradictory phenomenon, debilitating for the capitalist economy in the long run. But if neo-conservatives see the solution in winding down the welfare state, curtailing democracy and returning to purer forms of market capitalism Marxists look beyond capitalism for a lasting solution to its ills. The essence of the Marxist position seems to be that while the functional necessities of capitalism and the exigencies of class conflict have led to greater state involvement in the system, the latter in turn has contributed to the development of a new crisis. As Gough puts it: 'The welfare state is a product of the *contradictory* development of capitalist society and in turn it has generated new contradictions which every day become more apparent.'[11] The needs of capital, class struggle and contradictions seem to be the key Marxist concepts involved in understanding the development of the welfare state and its relationship to the current difficulties. Let us spell out the argument.

Marxists see the growth of the state and of social expenditure as important developments, but emphasise that the notion of the 'welfare state' is a form of mystification. The so-called welfare state is an integral part of modern capitalist society and must be analysed as such. Marxists see this relationship in terms of the functions performed by the state for the capitalist system. This radical functionalism is exemplified very well by writers such as James O'Connor. O'Connor's thesis has been influential among Marxists and neo-Marxists in connection with the understanding of the modern capitalist state, and merits close attention. He argues that the capitalist state must perform two basic functions: accumulation and legitimisation. The first refers broadly to economic functions, essentially those of ensuring profitability, investment and economic growth. The second refers to sociopolitical functions, those of ensuring that the capitalist social order appears a 'just', 'fair' and 'proper' system, and that social harmony is maintained.

In the conditions of advanced capitalist economy both functions have meant a much greater involvement of the state with civil society.[12] As Gamble and Walton point out, the Great Depression exposed the weaknesses inherent in un-regulated capitalism. It also led to intense conflict between labour and capital. During the 1930s it became apparent 'that the powers of the state had to be employed if high levels of output and employment, let alone growth, were to be assured.'[13] The state had to be more directly involved in the process of capitalist accumulation. In other words, maintaining demand through the use of fiscal and monetary instruments, providing infrastructural services for capital (e.g. education, research and development, roads, communications, subsidies to business, and the like) are a part of the accumulation function of the state which has expanded a great deal in the post-war years. If the accumulation function involves, directly or indirectly, 'productive' forms of state expenditure, the legitimisation function involves largely 'un-productive' expenditure (e.g. maintaining the dependent population) which contributes to social peace and fosters the idea of a caring state. These two factors are analytically distinct but empirically often intermingled. In fact, O'Connor suggests that 'nearly every state agency is involved in the accumulation and legitimisation functions and nearly every state expenditure has this two-fold character.'[14]

However, the development of the welfare state cannot be understood simply as a response to the functional necessities of capitalism. It is also a response to working-class pressure, an attempt to moderate the class struggle and maintain the overall conditions of capital accumulation and social harmony. Thus Marxists tend to see the post-war welfare state as a sort of political settlement between capital and labour. For Gough, not only the early post-war development but the growth in social expenditure in the 1960s and early 1970s was largely due to working-class pressure. Full employment increased the economic and political leverage of the organised working class to obtain improvements not only in money wages but also in the 'social wage'.[15]

The validity of this particular thesis about the influence of the working class is not at issue here. The main point is that the class struggle perspective to some extent counterbalances the functional approach. For example, to suggest that some of the welfare policies at least may have been forced upon the ruling class implies that they may represent a development detrimental rather that beneficial for capital. Moreover the growth of collective social provision in response to working-class pressure leaves open the possibility that social welfare may embody the logic of need-satisfaction which is quite different from the logic of market distribution of resources. It is this 'progressive' aspect of the social services that partly accounts for Marxist support for welfare despite its positive functions for capital. Overall, however, the Marxist argument is that it is the logic of capital that prevails. Gough points out that Marxists tend to 'veer towards one or the other' of two basic interpretations: some see 'the welfare state as a functional response to the needs of capital ... others see the welfare state as the unqualified fruits of the working-class struggle, as concessions wrested from an unwilling state.'[16] However most writers combine elements of both and the use of this formula (needs of capital plus class struggle equals welfare state) involves quite a bit of tight-rope walking (the welfare state is 'good' and 'bad' at the same time!). But we shall examine the implications of this duality a little later.

In Marxist theory the idea of institutional conflict and disequilibrium, in short the presence of dysfunctional tendencies within a social system, is indicated by the notion of 'contradiction'. It is contradiction that provides the counterpoint to functional integration of the social system in Marxist theory. Thus capitalism is not only a relatively integrated structure but also contains in-built contradictions. Perhaps the two most important of these are (a) between the forces and the relations of production, and (b) between the social nature of production and the private nature of appropriation. The first points to the imbalance between increasing productive capacity on the one hand and the unplanned, anarchic, profit-oriented nature of capitalist production on the other. Booms and slumps are an expression of this fundamental disjunction. The second contradiction is indicated by the imbalance of an increasingly co-operative, collective and communal process of social production which is nevertheless carried on within the framework of private ownership, appropriation and control. The distributional conflict between profits and wages resulting

in strikes, etc. (i.e. class conflict) expresses this contradiction.

Now as far as increasing state intervention in the economy is
concerned the nub of the Marxist argument is this: whilst it
has been developed in order to counteract the effect of these
basic contradictions and succeeds in this objective temporarily, in the long run it fails. Why? Because it attempts to
overcome the effect of these contradictions without altering
the basic properties of the system. In these circumstances state
intervention can only postpone the crisis of capitalism which
must erupt sooner or later.[17] The post-war welfare state
managed to stave off the crisis of capitalism for more than two
decades. State intervention, in particular the welfare state,
developed in the first place to overcome structural weaknesses
of capitalism, has in turn become a problem for the capitalist
economy. The 'solution' itself has turned into a problem. This
in essence is the Marxist interpretation of the current crisis of
welfare capitalism.[18] Let us examine it in some detail.

O'Connor's important work *The Fiscal Crisis of the State*
tries to show how the entire process of state intervention within
the context of a liberal capitalist society is shot through with
contradictions. First, the two major functions of the state,
accumulation and legitimisation, are themselves often conflicting – pulling in different directions as it were. Second,
while the scope of state activity and hence also expenditure has
increased a great deal the state has to depend on the private
sector – individual and corporate – for its revenue (taxation).
This results in 'a tendency for state expenditures to increase
more rapidly than the means of financing them' – what
O'Connor describes as the 'fiscal crisis' of the state.[19] This
fiscal gap, or budget deficit, has of course grown much
more acute since O'Connor's book was published in 1973.
Third, given the plural, interest-group form of the polity
government policies are determined largely through the workings of the political market. The result is 'private appropriation of state power for particularistic ends' as well as 'a
great deal of waste, duplication and overlapping of state
projects and services'.[20] Both exacerbate the fiscal crisis. In
sum, the process of state intervention, including the growth
of the state budget, is highly contradictory and in the long

run weakens the system's capacity for producing economic surplus.

In a broad sense O'Connor's thesis that accumulation and legitimisation often make conflicting demands on the state is true. But it is more in the nature of a half-truth. Briefly, he seems to be saying that there is an inherent conflict between the economic and the social welfare functions of the state. The former must aim at serving the needs of private capital, for example by helping to increase the rate of return on capital, providing opportunity for profitable investment, offering incentives through the tax system for risk-taking enterprise, encouraging labour mobility, and the like. Social welfare, on the other hand, which has to do with legitimisation, requires the government to strive towards fairness, equity, justice, and the like. For example, it calls for a progressive system of taxation, adequate social protection and the regulation of industry in the interests of workers. Such measures are not likely to help capitalist accumulation.

Marxist critics of O'Connor have already pointed out that accumulation and legitimisation functions are not only con-flicting but are also – and meant to be – mutually supportive.[21] This point needs to be developed more fully. The Keynesian and the Beveridgian aspects of the post-war welfare state were meant to complement each other. Thus, full employment policies were meant to help accumulation or economic growth by maintaining demand and a high level of output. They were also expected to help in keeping unemployment insurance schemes solvent. At the same time full employment policies were also to have a pay-off in terms of legitimising capitalism. And this is more or less how they seem to have worked, at any rate in Western Europe, for the best part of the post-war years. Again, welfare policies such as unemployment compensation and old age pensions, were on the one hand meant as legiti-misation, and on the other hand were also to help accumu-lation, i.e. maintain purchasing power and act as counter-cyclical devices. Now no one would deny that the logic of either accumulation or legitimisation *carried beyond a certain point* would begin to conflict with that of the other. And no doubt at the moment the problem of reconciling the 'economic' and 'social' objectives seems particularly acute. Yet the success of welfare capitalism in the 1950s and 1960s showed that economic growth and social welfare are not necessarily conflicting goals. What O'Connor points to are largely *tendencies*, such as inflation and rising rates of taxation, connected with the legitimisation function which may be detrimental for the economy. But this does not imply a *necessary* conflict between these two aims. Nonetheless, O'Connor's detailed analysis of crisis tendencies draws attention to the dysfunctional aspects of the relation between the 'economic' and the 'social', a problem that had become much more acute by the late 1970s.

O'Connor's analysis of the 'fiscal crisis' of the state is however much more convincing. The state is expected to take responsibility for many things (economic and social) yet it has no direct control over productive resources which remain largely in private hands. This is an important argument. It certainly pinpoints a 'structural' problem of the mixed economy. True, the state also owns some industries (the nationalised sector) in all western industrial countries. But industries have been acquired by the state for a wide variety of reasons (these vary from country to country, and from industry to industry), the least of which is to earn a surplus and provide a revenue base for the government.[22] In fact, many state undertakings are in the nature of public utilities (e.g. transport and gas and electricity supplies, run more or less as social services) and for sociopolitical reasons they are often run at a loss rather than made to pay their way. This is also true of many other state-owned enterprises.[23]

Be that as it may, O'Connor's argument holds. Economic surplus (profit) is produced mainly in the private sector (no matter how important the role of the public sector in making this possible) and income is distributed in the first place through the market mechanism. The state then 'conscripts' a part of this income (by taxation, etc.) to meet its own expenses. However this need not lead to fiscal crisis if the citizens (individuals and firms) pay up in taxes what they demand collectively of the government by way of services. But it does not work out that way. Here O'Connor's argument centres largely on the notion of fiscal irresponsibility – an argument that is practically identical with that of the new Right (see p. 38 above).

Every economic and social class and group wants government to spend more and more money on more and more things. But no one wants to pay new taxes or higher rates on old taxes. Indeed, nearly everyone wants lower taxes, and many groups have agitated successfully for tax relief.[24]

Milton Friedman? No, James O'Connor. And further, 'Society's demands on local and state budgets seemingly are unlimited, but people's willingness and capacity to pay for these demands appear to be narrowly limited. And at the federal level expenditures have increased significantly faster than the growth of total production.'[25] In other words O'Connor, like the ideologues of the new Right, and in a language surprisingly similar, is describing 'government overload', whose most visible sign is the budget deficit.

Let us however also note the difference between the two positions. For Marxists, state intervention has been 'necessary' to correct market failure and to moderate the class struggle. But this attempt has led capitalism into fresh contradictions. Here Marxists have the edge over the new Right whose explanation of the growth of the state as largely a result of misguided reformism or an accretion of short-term expediency is palpably weak. On the other hand, what Marxist argument tends to leave out of account, or at least plays down seriously, is the role of intellectual ideologies (e.g. Keynesianism) in encouraging budget deficit. For the new Right, it was Keynesianism that released the politicians from the constraints of 'sound finance' (the gold standard, balanced budgets, etc.) and greatly encouraged deficit financing (see Chapter 2). This is an important point. For clearly neither the 'need' for accumulation nor legitimisation of itself leads to budget deficit. As we know from the British experience of the 1930s, for example, the Depression did not 'lead' to an expanded government budget. Quite the opposite. The role of economic and other ideas – the 'definition of the situation' – is an important element in decision-making in this context. That the bourgeois state has been running budget deficits and has been living with the 'fiscal crisis' for quite a little while cannot be understood without taking the Keynesian legitimisation of deficits into account. Yet the 'materialist' emphasis of

Marxist theory crowds out the all-important role of ideas in social action. (This is quite different from the role of 'ideology' as a form of rationalisation and mystification on which Marxists tend to focus.)

O'Connor's final point, namely, the effect of the political market in expanding the state budget and in exacerbating the fiscal crisis, mirrors even more closely the new Right's allegations about government failure and government overload. For Hayek and Friedman the fiscal crisis has a lot to do with the way the sectional interests make use of the state for selfish ends (see pp. 30-1 above). For O'Connor too 'the fiscal crisis is exacerbated by the *private* appropriation of state power for *particularistic* ends' (emphasis added).[26] He notes that a host of '"special interests" – corporations, industries, regional and other business interests – make claims on the budget . . . organised labor and workers generally make various claims of different kinds of social consumption, and the unemployed and poor (together with businessmen in financial trouble) stake their claims.'[27] Here we seem to be a long way from the schematic interpretations of Marxist theory, functional necessities of capital or a bipolar class struggle. Rather, what O'Connor's refreshingly open-ended and empirical exposition depicts is a Hobbesian struggle in the political market-place, a series of 'unprincipled' demands placed by a variety of interests on the government resulting in overload. What is missing in such Marxist accounts is the new Right's emphasis on the effect of electoral competition among political parties in encouraging this overload.

Moreover, like most Marxists, O'Connor finds it difficult to escape functionalist and reified thinking. For example, he speaks of 'needs' in the same breath as he speaks of the demands made by various groups on the state for help: 'it is a fact that growing *needs* which only the state can meet create ever greater claims on the state budget' (emphasis added).[28] Examples of such needs? 'People who need government-provided services', 'corporations that want loans and subsidies' and 'government employees who need adequate income'.[29] Are these 'needs' really different from 'wants' that individuals or groups feel they may have? Can 'needs' be separated (and thus 'objectified') from the political process through which they are defined, articulated and met? The problem with O'Connor's approach is that his overall thesis is expressed in functional terms, namely that what the capitalist state does is to be understood in terms of fulfilling the function of accumulation and legitimisation. Yet his group-focused account of how the state budget actually grows takes a broad 'action frame of reference' which suggests that what the state responds to are selfish demands made by a variety of sectional interests. Clearly it would not do to suggest that every demand made by a corporation for loans or subsidy is a 'need' for accumulation, or that every demand made by a social group on the state represents a 'need' that must be met if legitimacy is to be maintained.

In fact, what O'Connor is implicitly concerned with is a conflict between the principles underlying the market economy and those underlying the plural polity, a conflict that is reflected in state policies. But this also suggests that the liberal capitalist state (and 'bourgeois' democracy) cannot be reduced to the functions of servicing the capitalist economy, a reductionism quite common in Marxist analysis. Indeed, O'Connor recognises that by itself 'interest-group politics is inconsistent with the survival and expansion of capitalism.'[30] Interests are particular and divergent and interest-consciousness leads to contradictory policies, 'making it difficult or impossible to plan the economy as a whole.'[31] Therefore to ensure that class interests of capital as a whole are safeguarded 'a class-conscious political directorate is needed.'[32] Marxists locate this more or less in the executive branch of the government, and in the state bureaucracy more generally. Budgetary control, including techniques such as the PPBS[33] for example, serves as a method of achieving this goal. However, O'Connor's analysis of the experience of the United States suggests that the attempt to mould something like a rational economic and social policy, from the viewpoint of the interest of capital as a whole (a somewhat elusive notion anyway), out of the shifting sands of interest-group politics and sectional interests achieves only limited success (note for example the failure of the PPBS). In short, Marxists, like the new Right, point to government failure which largely arises out of the vagaries of the political market. Not only does a policy rational from the viewpoint of capital prove elusive but 'there is a great deal of waste, duplication, and overlapping of state projects and services' since claims are made and processed through the political system. Overall the process of state intervention in the economy proves to be 'highly irrational . . . from the stand-point of administrative coherence, fiscal stability, and poten-tially profitable accumulation'.[34] We have focused on O'Connor's discussion of the crisis of the state largely because he remains virtually the only Marxist writer (in the English language) who deals with the contradictions and crisis of the post-wear capitalist *state* in detail.

O'Connor's focus was on the fiscal crisis. More recent Marxist writers have extended the scope of their exploration to the economic crisis of welfare capitalism. Marxists differ amongst themselves a good deal on how they see the crisis and the part played by the welfare state in it. Perhaps most would agree with Gough's observation that the growth of the welfare state 'is neither cause nor consequence of capitalist develop-ment, but one aspect of it. Consequently it is neither cause nor consequence of the present crisis, but again one aspect of it.'[35] None the less, most Marxists, including Gough, recognise that the growth of the welfare state (both in its nature and scope) has contributed handsomely to the current difficulties of capitalist economy. Thus it is generally believed that the full employment policies of the post-war years combined with improved unemployment compensation and social security provision strengthened the position of labour and enabled it to win wage advances. Business, on the other hand, is subject to international competition and could not pass on the costs in higher prices, especially from about the later 1960s onwards. The result has been a gradual squeeze on profits so much so that by the late 1970s the conditions for investment and capitalist growth had been seriously weakened. In particular, countries with a low growth of productivity and a militant, well-organised labour force – notably Britain – have seen a dramatic decline in profitability. Since the welfare state did not in any way change capitalist *relations* of production (e.g. the cash nexus and the inherent conflict underlying the capital-labour relations) in the long run it ended up undermining capital's profitability. The presence of the 'reserve army of labour' (the unemployed) and the ability of capital to depress wages, especially in times of recession, are the normal means of restoring profitability. But the 'very success . . . of post-war governments in maintaining full employment and moderating the [trade] cycle meant that yet another automatic regulator of capitalism was dispensed with.'[36]

The growth of the state, and of the social welfare sector in particular, has also made inroads into capital's health. Here the relevant economic arguments are exceedingly involved and Gough, for example, deals quite comprehensively with many of these.[37] The simplistic notion that public employment and expenditure, in short the state sector, grows at the expense of the private sector is untenable. Marxists point out, for example, that transfer payments (a large part of social expenditure), such as retirement pensions, simply shuffle cash around and the money is spent in buying *private* goods and services. Expenditure on the health services again involves the purchase (by health authorities or the consumer) of drugs, appliances, equipment and the like from the private sector. None the less, on balance it would seem that a large state sector can draw resources (capital and manpower) away from the private sector which alone produces economic surplus (profit) and also goods and services for export. Here again the arguments of the Left bear a close resemblance to those of the Right – both see social expenditure largely as an 'unproductive' burden on capitalist economy.

Theories of inflation are probably as plentiful as economists themselves. Marxists among economists are no exception.[38] But it is safe to say that for the Marxist inflation is more a symptom of the crisis of welfare capitalism than a cause. In part it reflects a situation where the state, the employers and the workers all insist on maintaining their share of a shrinking 'pie'. The growth of the state sector has, in the post-war years, been partly financed through increasing the money supply. With the onset of recession the revenue base has shrunk while expenditure has, if anything, tended to grow (e.g. through larger outlay on unemployment benefits, aid to industries in difficulty) resulting in larger deficits and inflation. As Gamble and Walton put it, 'Once accumulation began to falter, the burden of high wages and state spending became too great.

Inflation was one result.'[39] Yet inflation is 'only a symptom of the real crisis. The real crisis is caused by the obstacles that now stand in the way of further growth and expansion in the framework of a capitalist economy.'[40] Inflation gets worse as governments try to expand the money supply and credit to finance their own expenditure and maintain prosperity so that goods produced by industry can be shold at a profit. The impasse in which the mixed economy and the welfare state find themselves – involving inflation, recession, unemployment and budget deficit – cannot be broken without altering the parameters (economic and political) of the post-war consensus.

Increasingly, recent Marxist writings note a shift towards the policy of retrenching social expenditure, what Gunder Frank calls 'welfare farewell'.[41] With a prolonged crisis and no sign of recovery, capitalist states are trying to create unemployment (in order to exert a downward pressure on wages) besides introducing various austerity measures in the 'national interest'. Abandoning the commitment to full employment and dismantling the welfare state (some Marxists see a 'restructuring' rather than dismantling process taking place) are becoming the favoured policies; 'productive investment', beginning unabashedly with increased military expenditure is being given increasing priority.[42] Like Frank, Gough too offers sombre reflections. The solution of the economic crisis would involve weakening the power of labour organisations in order that the economic and 'social' wage might be reduced and profitability restored. In this process 'political democracy and the welfare state will both be vulnerable; their fate will be linked.'[43] Most Marxists would agree with this gloomy scenario.

Marxist Attitude to the Crisis of Welfare

By now it will be clear that Marxist assessments of the welfare state, unlike those of the new Right, are not one-sided. Marxists do not reject the social services, state commitment to full employment, and the like out of hand simply because they leave capitalist relations of production (and therefore the nature of society as a whole) unaltered. Social welfare may help shore up capitalism, materially and ideologically, but it also represents a gain for the working class in its struggle against exploitation. Thus Gough speaks of state welfare provision as a form of 'social wage'. Forms of collective provision, such as the National Health Service, social security, etc. 'do represent very important steps forward and do in part "enhance welfare".'[44] The welfare state represents a 'contradictory unity' and the Marxist has the somewhat daunting task of defending and condemning it at the same time. In the mid-1960s, when social expenditure was growing apace and the welfare state was synonymous with consensus politics, Marxists took on a radical stance. They 'exposed' the real nature of welfare in capitalist society, including its function as a mechanism of social control and as a means of incorporation of the working class. Now that the political centre of gravity has moved to the right and the welfare state is under attack Marxists are coming forward to defend it as a form of collective social provision and as a part of working-class living standards.

In any case the corollary to the Marxist belief that class struggle has played a major part in the development of the welfare state is the idea that working-class action is crucial in its defence. For the best part of the post-war years it was a firm belief, not only in radical but also in bourgeois and moderate Left circles, that any attempt to tamper with the 'gains' of the working class, (e.g. full employment and universal social services) would bring about swift retribution. First, it was believed that such a government would be punished electorally, and second that such action would probably result in serious disorder and social instability. These prognoses were by no means ill-founded or exaggerated. In fact the broad electoral popularity of the policies of full employment and social welfare was the basis of the party political consensus on these issues. Undoubtedly, a political party in office that had been seen as creating unemployment or actively dismantling the social services would have faced electoral disaster in the 1950s and 1960s. As for the extra-parliamentary response of the masses to such policies this was largely a matter of conjecture since the post-war years had seen little by way of direct action. None the less, the 'events' of May 1968 in France were a reminder that manual workers had by no means been 'domesticated' by bourgeois democracy. In Britain the action of the miners in 1973-4 against the Conservative government's pay policies, and the resulting confrontation, showed the potential for working-class resistance to unfavourable policies. But more generally the increased strength of the trade union movement (at least in Western Europe), the entrenchment of social rights in post-war western society, and the experience of the 1930s suggested the likelihood of strong opposition – parliamentary or otherwise – to anti-welfare policies.

As western economies moved into rampant inflation accompanied with cuts in social services and growing unemployment Marxists expected the class struggle to intensify and working-class militancy to increase. In the aftermath of the miners' strike and the election of a labour government, Gough wrote, 'Britain has entered its most critical post-war crisis with the organisational and political strength of the working class at a new height and the bourgeois political order in a state of unprecedented disarray.'[45] Writing in a mood of radical optimism he thought that the attempt to impose a wage freeze or substantial unemployment would be 'vigorously resisted'. Meanwhile, with the forces opposed to cuts in social expenditure 'gaining strength', the crisis would lead to a 'decisive test of strength'.[46]

Subsequent developments have not borne out these prognostications. Indeed, the irony of the situation is that at the depth of Britain's crisis the electorate (including large sections of the working class) put a Conservative government, pledged to radical right-wing policies, in office. But more disturbing still, from a Marxist perspective, is the acquiescence of the masses to the very high level of unemployment. It was a widely-held belief in Britain, until the mid-1970s, that anything like a million unemployed would lead to riots and other disturbances. Britain now has over 3 million unemployed and apart from some anti-police violence among youth there is little sign of protest, let alone disorder. But as perceptive neo-Marxists such as Habermas recognise, the very existence of social programmes – unemployment benefit and social security, the health services, and the like – helps cushion the impact of the economic crisis.[47]

Overall, however, Marxists find the working-class response to the economic crisis disheartening. As Rustin points out, in Britain as well as 'most other capitalist states beset by recession', the decline of the mixed economy 'has engendered so far not a tougher-minded general militancy of the Left, but a politics of retrenchment and narrow self-interest.'[48] More generally, Marxists cannot fail to recognise that the collapse of the political Centre has benefited so far not the Left but the Right, as shown for example by the election of the Thatcher and Reagan governments. But in one respect Marxists are now in a better position to make sense of such political response to economic difficulties. Many appreciate the 'relatively autonomous' role of politics and ideology in social action. Crass economism, such as the assumption that a worsening economic situation would of itself lead to radical left-wing action, is happily becoming rare.

All the same the political success of the new Right in a number of countries, and the appeal of its ideology more generally, is an aspect of the crisis that needs explaining. Marxists have tried to explain this, by and large, in terms of the 'populist' rhetoric and ideology of the new Right which builds on anti-collective and anti-statist sentiments. The contradictory nature of social democracy and its actions have a lot to do with this.[49] For, on the one hand, social democracy represents working-class aspirations and interests but on the other hand, it does so within the confines of the capitalist system. It has to 'discipline' the workers and their organisations. Instead of class interests it has to emphasise 'national interest', and instead of class relationships stress the relation between the government and the 'people'. These contradictions of social democracy become particularly acute in times of economic recession and the Right takes full advantage of it. Moreover, in extending the scope of the state, including in respect of welfare provision, social democracy has seen the state as more or less a neutral or benevolent institution. Expansion of the state has therefore become synonymous with the extension of socialism, a socialism which makes no attempt to mobilise democratic power at the grass roots. But without the latter, writes Hall, 'the state is increasingly encountered and experienced by ordinary working people as, indeed, not a beneficiary but a powerful bureaucratic imposition.'[50] Right-wing populism has exploited these contradictions so that while social democracy is associated with the Big State the new Right is out there 'with the people'.

The idea that the Right has been able to discredit the welfare state because of social democracy's defaults is a continuing refrain in Marxist writing. Corrigan, for example, speaks of the 'bureaucratic state form' of the social services. The mass of the working people 'have experienced education, supplementary benefit, the NHS, council housing etc., as something external and bureaucratic. Over thirty years this has turned significant sections of the population away from the welfare state as a progressive set of institutions.'[51] While the first part of Corrigan's statement seems unobjectionable, in the last sentence he makes a truly astonishing assertion for which he offers no evidence. Moreover, Corrigan is totally mistaken when he writes that 'many of the Tory votes were votes *against* the welfare state.'[52] Whatever else they may have been, the Tory votes were not in any sense against the welfare state. Two pieces of evidence are important here. First, opinion polls in Britain (as well as in the USA) taken both before and after Thatcher's accession to power show a high level of support for the social services and for government action more generally in maintaining equity and fairness.[53] Bureaucratic the state services may be, as Hall and Corrigan for example rightly point out, but it does not follow that this has necessarily affected public (including working-class) support for them. Second, it must be remembered that what the Tories in Britain promised in their election campaign was not a reduction in the *services* but in *wasteful public expenditure*. This was to be done by cutting out unnecessary work and employment ('bureaucracy'), reducing general extravagance in government, and making public services more efficient.

But an important winning point in the Tory election campaign was the promise to reduce taxes.[54] Surprisingly, British Marxists, possibly in their eagerness to escape economistic thinking, seemed to have paid scant attention to this point. For they are well aware of the contradiction of welfarism, namely that while the social services help maintain living standards, it is the masses, none the less, that have to pay for them. It is no secret that over the years governments of all complexions have increased the tax burden on working people very considerably.[55] The promise of a reduction in income taxes therefore has considerable appeal for the masses especially in times of stagnating personal incomes. Again, to respond to the electoral appeal of lower taxes is not necessarily to opt for the retrenchment of social expenditure. The contradiction in popular attitudes of 'having your cake and eating it too' comes out clearly in polls where individuals support tax reduction and at the same time demand higher government spending on major social services. In any case we may point out in this connection that to treat social welfare provision as a 'social wage' (as some Marxists seem to do) could be very misleading. For this suggests that the 'social wage' is an *addition* to the 'economic wage' of the working class, whereas the fact of the matter is that part of the economic wage is taken away from the workers and then returned (to the workers and others) in the form of social services.

Clearly there is a trade-off between economic and social welfare and the appeal of more take home pay cannot be ignored when considering the electoral success of the new Right. Indeed, it is no coincidence that in the United States, where tax revolts symbolised by Proposition 13 in California were very prominent in the late 1970s (see p. 51 above), Marxists emphasise the appeal of reduced taxes in explaining the Reagan victory.[56] Taxation, it is true, has not been a focal issue in Britain and nothing dramatic, even remotely approaching Propositon 13, has occurred in that respect. None the less, the undercurrent of dissatisfaction with the rising tax burden cannot be dismissed as unimportant (or worse still as a sign of 'bourgeois individualism'). In short, reducing taxation and eliminating 'waste' in government are attractive slogans to many working-class taxpayers in conditions of recession.

More important still in explaining the success of the new Right is another economic factor also largely ignored by Marxists. It is simply that the new Right's ideology of monetarism and anti-statism has gained credibility in the wake of the failure of Keynesianism and the mixed economy in the 1970s. Thanks to the deepening crisis of the capitalist economy, the Butskellism of the Heath, Wilson and Callaghan governments, incomes policies of various kinds, *ad hoc* measures for moderating wage demands and controlling inflation, such as the social contract – in short the Keynesian and neo-Keynesian nostrums have been tried over and over again, but without success. Since none of the old remedies seems to have worked, and the economy has remained trapped in the vicious circle of inflation, unemployment, wage restraint and economic stagnation the new, and instant, remedies proposed by the radical Right had considerable appeal.

A broadly similar situation existed in the United States where, of course, the legitimacy of the welfare state and the government more generally is weaker. In other words, we must dismiss the notion that the political victory of the new Right represents a turning away on the part of the masses from the welfare state and the mixed economy. And if that is true then it would not do to blame the bureaucratic form of the state services or the failure of social democracy to involve the masses for the new Right's popularity (however valid such criticism might be from a *socialist* perspective). Since, in the West as a whole, the mixed economy and Keynesianism had palpably failed, the time was ripe for a turn to other options – the policies of the radical Right. The more important question from the Marxist viewpoint, namely why the shift has been to the Right rather than Left, raises issues that cannot be broached here. My main point is that despite many weaknesses of the welfare state, its bureaucratism, professional dominance, minimal redistribution, to name but a few, it has neither lost its attraction for the masses (see p. 51 above) nor can it in any direct sense be held responsible for the success of the new Right.

A final point is this: Marxist writers on welfare tend to focus on the social services or the Beveridgian aspect of the welfare state. From the standpoint of the masses however, it was the Keynesian aspect of the post-war welfare state (i.e. full employment and steady economic growth) that was more important. It was above all the combination of plentiful jobs – not only ensuring steady employment for the male wage earner but also enabling wives to supplement the family wage – and economic growth, in short the 'affluent society', that was the cornerstone of the post-war policy consensus. The 'welfare state' rounded off this prosperity with a measure of security and equity. What the economic difficulties of the 1970s have done is to drive a wedge between the Keynesian (economic) and Beveridgian (social) aspects of welfare. It is this rift that the new Right has exploited, making social welfare the scapegoat for the failure of the economy. Ironically, not unlike the Marxists, it is the new Right that has been emphasising the primacy of production over consumption, of economic growth over social distribution. Put in this form the new Right has a convincing argument – economic growth led by the private sector and 'real' productive employment are the foundations of western prosperity: by encroaching too far upon the economy the welfare state (essentially distributive) has undermined these foundations and must therefore be rolled back. Put in this form (i.e. as a matter of *priorities*), cutbacks in social consumption (to match reduced personal consumption and incomes generally) make sense. In short the economic difficulties of welfare capitalism have provided the new Right with the soil in which its brand of populism can take root.

This does not mean that people have turned away from the values of progressive liberalism (USA) or social democracy (Western Europe). Rather the broad aspirations of the people remain the same – jobs, government provision of services, prosperity coupled with security and equity. It is rather that the tried and tested methods of the last twenty-five years do not work. The new Right's approach is therefore seen as a new *means* to broadly similar ends. The electoral strategy of the new Right, both in the UK and the USA, would seem to corroborate this. For example, in the United States 'the success of Reagan and other conservative candidates in the industrial states' was in no small measure due to the 'accentuation of the pro-growth aspects of the supply side programme.'[57] In Britain the Thatcher government rode to power on the wave of a strong reaction against the unions resulting from the 'winter of discontent' (widespread strikes to back large wage demands). Disciplining the unions was a part of the Tory election pledge. But the Tories also emphasised the positive aspects of their policy, especially economic growth. This was to be brought about by lowering taxes and so releasing incentives, curbing excessive consumption (private and public) and more generally by attending to production.[58] Of course, the massive unemployment created by the Thatcher government is quite the opposite of the promise of economic revival and the creation of 'real' jobs in the private sector (in place of massive and growing public employment). The Reagan government too has little to show by way of economic recovery. It remains true none the less that in both cases the emphasis has been on *production* – on economic growth rather than distribution.

The emphasis on economic growth (in Marxist terms 'accumulation') raises an important question. Alan Wolfe, an American Marxist writes, 'The political success of the American right raises a number of questions, none of them easily resolved by any of the prevailing Marxist theories of the state.'[59] And he asks: 'What happens when an administration opts for accumulation and allows legitimation to take care of itself?'[60] This way of posing the problem highlights the weakness of the Marxist (O'Connor's) thesis which counterposes the legitimisation function of the state to its accumulation function. In fact *accumulation is one of the major sources of legitimisation of the capitalist system.*

Let me explain. What is capital accumulation from the Marxist (functionalist) standpoint is simply economic growth from the viewpoint of the masses. And surely the trump card of capitalism has been that it is a great engine of prosperity and efficiency and that sooner or later its benefits spread to all sections of the population (in Kennedy's much-quoted phrase 'a rising tide lifts all boats'). The new Right's emphasis on 'getting the economy right' is therefore not necessarily at the cost of legitimisation. Not only economic growth but also individual liberties and political democracy – with all that they entail – are important sources of legitimacy for modern capitalism. True, the new Right's position remains highly ambivalent on individual and political liberties (see pp. 60-1 above) but, on the whole, monetarism and the free-market ideology tend to be libertarian in stance. They are against state direction and for voluntarism, against incomes policies and for market determination of wages and prices, against import controls (in principle at any rate) and for free trade.

In any case, the important point to be kept in mind is that the state's welfare activities constitute only one among several major sources of legitimacy of post-war capitalism. Therefore the scope for restricting or even retrenching the social services if that would permit other sources of support for the system, notably economic growth and political liberties, to be maintained is greater than Marxists believe. It is in this sense that the dichotomy of 'accumulation' versus 'legitimisation' as contradictory functions can be particularly misleading. 'Production' (whether capitalist or otherwise) *is* really important in all societies and in the name of getting production right all sorts of sacrifices can be imposed on the masses, at least temporarily, by the ruling élites. Moreover if we note that not only workers and other subordinate groups but also sections of capital seem to be adversely affected (through bankruptcies, business failure, and the like) then the wider significance of the 'accumulation' approach becomes clear. It is an attempt to bring back society – workers and capitalists alike – to the basic ground rules of capitalism, namely, living by the market principle for the sake of future prosperity. Clearly, if the new Right cannot deliver – and this is most likely – then the electorate may once again turn to the political Centre ('New Centre'?) as support for the Liberal-Social Democratic alliance in Britain, for example, suggests. The situation remains far more fluid than many recent Marxist analyses, focused on the retreat of social democracy and the advance of the new Right, suggest. At any rate, the mass of the people in western societies have not rejected the welfare state nor, I would suggest, the value mix represented by social democracy. It is simply that workers seem to value *economic* welfare as well as social welfare, individualism and liberty (which includes the right to strike and free collective bargaining) as well as collectivism and security, and it would be a mistake to exaggerate the importance of social welfare in the wider context of values and preferences.

Finally, we have to consider the political implications of the Marxist view of the welfare crisis. One fairly obvious, if somewhat academic, conclusion would be that since the so-called welfare state is a part of the larger capitalist system the pursuit of welfare in capitalist society is the labour of Sisyphus. For not only does the system limit the nature and scope of 'genuine' welfare but since it is founded on insoluble contradictions, which must sooner or later give rise to serious economic crises (as at present), the material basis of welfare provision always remains at risk. A stable system of social welfare cannot be built on the quicksands of capitalist economy. The lasting solution to these contradictions is therefore socialism. However for Marxists, as they are well aware, problems just begin rather than end with that conclusion. I shall take up this question of the socialist solution later. A second, and rather less fundamentalist conclusion, is suggested, for example, by Gough. In a political postscript to his analysis of the welfare state he writes that if his 'arguments have any validity they must be capable of translation into political strategy.'[61] Once

the contradictory nature of the welfare state and its contradictory impact on capitalism is appreciated, then the political strategy of all who work in it, use it or are concerned with it can be refined. The positive aspects of welfare policies need defending and extending, their negative aspects need exposing and attacking.[62]

In principle this is unobjectionable. But how do we separate the 'positive' from the 'negative'? Gough's answer is that the concept of 'human needs' becomes relevant at this point in making this distinction.[63] These conclusions are in line with Gough's painstaking, systematic and largely undogmatic analysis of the welfare state. But the result is an approach of an 'on the one hand' and 'on the other hand' variety which fails to clarify the overall Marxist attitude to the crisis of welfare capitalism. Gough considers the various options available within the confines of capitalism for dealing with the crisis, namely monetarism and market orientation as well as corporatism and social contract approach. He has no difficulty in showing that these strategies are unlikely to be workable either because they would have to rely on repression or because they would have to secure co-operation from labour in conditions of economic recession and the absence of growth.[64] This 'negative' stance leaves the aim of Gough's political postscript rather unclear. In so far as it reminds the reader of the dual nature of welfare in capitalist society it is useful. His main point, namely the need to struggle for more 'progressive' social policies within welfare capitalism, also remains valid. What remains unresolved, indeed unaddressed, is the thorny problem of the 'part-whole' relationship and its implications. Thus if social welfare is inextricably a part of the larger, capitalist system then its 'good' features cannot really be separated from the 'bad' ones.

The current difficulties of welfare capitalism make this abundantly clear. For example, if today the social services are to be maintained at their current level (the 'social wage') then given the constraints of capitalist production ('profits') this may have to be done at the cost of the economic wage. Corporatism and social contractarian approaches are based largely on such a premise. But clearly this is a compromise which accepts capitalist production as given and therefore subordinates (at least temporarily) the values of welfare to the logic of profitability. Thus within the confines of capitalism the 'good' in social welfare can only be maintained by catering to the 'bad' capitalistic elements (e.g. ensuring that the welfare system aids rather than hinders production, that it seeks to be efficient, cost-conscious and the like). The alternative to such a compromise or collusion with the capitalist economy is to oppose cuts in welfare in a purely *ad hoc* and defensive manner disregarding the implications of social expenditure for the capitalist economy as a whole. And this is more or less what Marxist and other radical activists seem to be doing. But it is quite clear that what is gained on the swings of the social services can easily be lost on the roundabouts of unemployment and low economic wages. In short, any attempt to deal with the 'part' raises the problem of the 'whole' which the dualistic approach to welfare fails to grapple with. Thus it is far from clear whether Gough considers the Welfare State *as a social system* – comprised of the mixed economy, social welfare and a plural polity – worth defending and fighting for. He fails to offer any clear strategy of how this might be done and *why* it should be done under the present circumstances.

Nevertheless, Gough can hardly be blamed for failing to resolve what has been a classical dilemma for Marxists in capitalist society, namely to support reformism is to 'dirty one's hands', to run the risk of class collaboration and, in the long run, harbour illusions about capitalism. On the other hand, to reject reforms altogether is to repudiate the role and potential of the working class in changing society. Perhaps Taylor-Gooby and Dale go to the heart of the matter in arguing that in the 'present context of capitalist crisis any strategy for defending and extending the social services which is not part and parcel of developing and organising around a programme for socialism will find it difficult to make headway.'[65]

In the following section I consider the argument for socialism as well as some of the major weaknesses of Marxist theory in relation to the crisis of welfare.

Marxist Socialism and Welfare

It was suggested that the key Marxist concepts involved in the analysis of the welfare state are the needs of capital, class struggle and contradictions. In discussing O'Connor's work I offered some criticism of the 'needs of capital' or the radical functionalist approach. Here I would like to consider some of the problems raised by the notion of class struggle and contradictions. Finally, I shall touch on some issues related to the 'socialist' solution.

In essence the Marxist notion of class struggle may be said to refer to the concerted action of workers in furthering their interests in capitalist society. This action may be aimed at the state or at employers. As a result of the class struggle capitalists make various concessions to workers. These represent working-class 'gains' within capitalism. The welfare state represents such a gain. Given the two-class model, with workers as the exploited class, Marxists tend to evaluate social reforms in terms of *workers*' interests – whether they enhance their life-chances, give them greater control over what affects their lives, and the like. In recent years, feminists have challenged this narrow Marxist view of welfare in capitalist society. Thus Wilson writes, 'the class struggle that obtained the Factory Acts and the Beveridge Plan could certainly not be said to have operated in the interest of women who were in both cases defined as home-bound individuals dependent on a male bread-winner.'[66] She points out that the concept of 'class struggle' cannot deal with the feminist critique of welfare provision which 'raises uncomfortable problems for those who seek to stress the role of working class demands.'[67] Taylor-Gooby and Dale try to resolve this problem by extending the notion of class struggle to include the challenge to 'capitalist oppression' – posed by 'oppressed groups' other than the workers, e.g. sexual, national and racial groups.[68] Whether class struggle is the appropriate term for these various interest-group activities (presumably the sexually-oppressed groups could include gay people, who could also then be seen as participating in the class struggle?) remains very much an open question. At least if all these oppressed groups were fighting against *capitalist* oppression there might be some justification in using the concept in this way. But to take women as an example – it is far from clear to feminists and others whether the 'enemy' is capitalism or patriarchy, i.e. a structure of oppression in which the working-class male finds himself on the side of capitalism and against women. The point is that there are so many 'oppressed' groups – interest groups struggling to change some aspect of society or the other – that to extend the notion of class struggle to cover all these denudes the concept of its scientific and analytic value. None the less, what Taylor-Gooby and Dale recognise indirectly is that a theory of socialist welfare which confines itself to the interests of male manual workers alone is far from adequate.

A different problem connected with the notion of class struggle is that the working class cannot be seen simply as a homogeneous group with identical interests. This is particularly important in the context of welfare which is connected with issues of life-chances and distribution. Thus Ginsburg speaks of working-class ambivalence towards state welfare. The labour movement has had a healthy suspicion of the state apparatus. The Liberal government's social insurance measures, for example, were distrusted, as they posed a 'threat to the tradition of working-class co-operative welfare exemplified by the friendly societies'.[69] Ginsburg believes that these societies have been much maligned in the social administration tradition as opponents of state welfare programmes. The point however is that the friendly societies largely recruited from the skilled artisan class.[70] For, on the whole, the lower working class had neither the security of employment nor the level of wages to be able to save regularly through friendly societies. Liberal reform measures were, in part, addressed to this problem.[71] In fact the Victorian working class was clearly divided into several strata with the skilled artisans (the 'labour aristocracy') largely able to finance their own insurance but not so the other layers of the working class. This status differentiation among workers must be taken into account if the complex relationship between welfare and the working class is to be understood fully. Perhaps O'Connor is alone among Marxist writers on the welfare state to distinguish between various groups of workers – workers in the corporate sector, the competitive sector, and so on. Like the 'fractions of capital' the 'fractions of labour' also need to be understood more adequately in relation to welfare. To speak of the working class as an undifferentiated category tends to obscure these differences and introduces an ambiguity in Marxist analysis that can be quite misleading.

In fact Marxist analyses differ a good deal in their assessment of the relationship between the working class and the welfare state. Gough and Ginsburg, for example, speak of the 'working class' or 'labour' (as opposed to capital) as a monolithic group engaged in a conflict against capital, in respect of taxation and welfare.[72] O'Connor on the other hand sees the situation in a different light.

The economic and political struggle around the issues of the distribution of the tax burden, the volume of state expenditures, and budgetary priorities have pitted interest group against interest group, white-collar suburbanite against city dweller, white worker against black worker, taxpayer against state worker, state worker against labour in the monopoly sector, and so on. Struggles within and against the state have not been fought along class lines and hence do not necessarily pose any serious political threat to the established social order. In fact, many of these struggles have polarized the working class.[73]

On the other side of the Atlantic Westergaard and Resler echo this:

The impact of social services had tended...to be divisive: to draw lines between different categories of workers...social security provisions distinguish 'the poor' from others; those who are given special help ... from those who use only the standard services. That by itself is liable to foster mutual resentments.[74]

Here again we see a 'contradiction' at work. Historically, workers' struggle has helped establish social welfare provision. The latter in turn appears to have served to fragment rather than unite workers. Whether the recent attack on state welfare provision (the impact of social services cuts and changes in taxation is always more or less specific) will help to unite all workers is a moot point. Be that as it may, the notion of sectional interest and division among workers in respect of the welfare state, as in respect of economic issues generally, seems a useful corrective to an over-schematised notion of a conflict between capital and labour. Overall, the problem of relating issues in welfare with sectional interests and demands on the one hand and wider class orientations and perspectives on the other remains unresolved in Marxist literature. Perhaps we could illustrate this further with reference to professional groups in the social services.

Marxist welfare analysis remains ambivalent in respect of the professional and social service bureaucracies. Thus Gough recognises that the growth of the social services has 'created a new and powerful force with a vested interest in the future development of welfare services'.[75] What is not clear is whether the attempt on the part of these vested interests, especially professionals and civil servants, to negotiate generous salaries, pension arrangements, better service conditions, and the like, thus swelling the social budget and establishing professional dominance more firmly, is welcome to the Marxist. In this connection Gough recognises that professionalism is a 'double-edged sword'.[76] But on the whole he takes a charitable view of the professions (e.g. doctors, teachers, social workers and others), arguing that their autonomy and control over work is threatened by the demands of the capitalist state for greater managerial control and accountability.[77] What is missing in his account is any perception of the conflict between professional power and privilege (often a form of monopoly power) on the one hand, and the public interest or client interest on the other. Overall, the relationship of state employment to the question of social welfare and the current crisis of capitalism remains somewhat unclarified in Marxist literature.[78] It must be recognised, however, that this is a problem with wide economic (e.g. productive/unproductive labour), sociological (e.g. class differentiation and class affiliation), and political (e.g. state employees as a vested interest and as a bulwark for the social services) ramifications and has yet to receive the attention if deserves.

The Marxist notion of contradiction and its relevance to the economic crisis has already been discussed. To recap: first, the capitalist market economy is a form of anarchy and in this sense has disequilibrium built into it. Second, private ownership of capital creates a class of non-owners and the ensuing conflict between wages and profits is also integral to the capitalist economy. These basic contradictions and conflicts are of course extremely serious and their implications can hardly be exaggerated. But the basic question is this: Does the presence of contradiction and conflict within a social system *ipso facto* imply a form of pathology? In other words, is a society free of contradictions and conflicts to be seen as the 'norm'? Is such a society possible and desirable? The Marxist answer to these questions seems to be a definite yes. Socialism will presumably be a system free of inherent contradictions and conflicts.

Be that as it may, at least as far as 'actually existing socialism' (i.e. the Soviet or Chinese-style society) is concerned, it has its own contradictions and conflicts. Group conflicts remain latent because of the totalitarian state form of these societies but erupt with great violence and intensity from time to time, leading to renewed forms of bureaucratic domination. It would seem that all complex social systems contain within them the sources of a wide variety of contradictions and conflicts.[79] Thus it may be more a question of exchanging one set of contradictions and conflicts for another, rather than being able to devise a society free of contradictions and conflicts. Yet implicit in Marxist exposition of the contradictions of capitalism is the image of a socialist Utopia (a harmony of interests and perfect integration of institutions) that bears little relation to any conceivable reality. The notion that a society with 'inherent' contradictions is somehow a society with a fatal flaw in its structure, and therefore requires a total change of structure, would seem largely utopian. Up to a point the presence of contradictions and conflicts in a society can be seen as a sign of health rather than pathology. This is not only because they are the major sources of social change in complex societies and therefore may be regarded as 'normal' features, it is also because contradictions and conflicts represent the negative aspect of a duality (contradiction within contradiction?) which also has a positive aspect. Thus the obverse of class conflict is free collective bargaining, absence of labour direction by the state, the right to strike, and the autonomy of trade unions. The obverse of capitalist contradiction is rapid economic growth, rising productivity and efficiency, and high standards of living for the masses in the long run. What we are confronted with is not a simple choice between 'good' or 'evil', 'black' or 'white', but a complex packaging of a set of good and evil which 'on the one hand' enhances well-being and 'on the other hand' also inflicts much suffering. In this sense not only the welfare state but capitalism too is a 'contradictory unity', an unstable coalition of good and evil.

If Marxism did not exist, it would certainly have to be invented. For it remains a necessary even if not a sufficient social theory, and is probably the best single theory available for a critical understanding of capitalist society. That is its major strength. But it is also a theory of socialism, of revolution and the building of a socialist society. That is its major weakness. In this, Marxist theory resembles some unfinished Renaissance statue with a powerful torso, a muscular, well-proportioned body hewn out of stone — but without a head. Let us follow the implications of this disproportion.

Implicit in Marxist critique of capitalism is the notion that capitalist society can be – indeed is destined to be – replaced by a socialist society, ushered in by the working class. This belief in progress and in socialism as the next 'higher stage' in social evolution is fundamental to Marxism. Without it, the critique of capitalism remains largely 'negative', a demolition job which cannot put anything better in place of capitalism. Yet it is as a theory of socialism (economic, political and social) that Marxism remains sadly inadequate. As we know, the 1930s fully vindicated the Marxist theory of contradictions and crisis as far as the capitalist economy was concerned. Yet nowhere in advanced capitalist society did workers embark on the path of revolution. True, the current crisis does not bear comparison (at least so far) with the dramatic economic crash and the acute social distress of the 1930s. None the less, given the strength of trade unions generally and the nature of expectations generated by affluent capitalism, a vigorous response on the part of the workers was expected. But this expectation has not been fulfilled and, as we have already noted, Marxists find the workers' response to the current crisis somewhat dispiriting. It is clear that the crisis of the mixed economy and the weakening of the Centre has benefited the Right rather than the Left, which finds itself in disarray. Few Marxists today harbour any illusions about the weakness of the Left. Thus while 'in theory' socialism remains the 'solution', in practice it proves as elusive as ever. As a result, the political implications of Marxism amount to little more than largely a defensive and reactive strategy of opposing cuts in social expenditure.

A fundamental weakness of the Marxist position in the West seems to be that it has not come to terms (perhaps it cannot) with the entire historical experience of 'actually existing' socialism. For I would like to suggest that one important reason why it has been easy for 'authoritarian populism' of the new Right to win support is that the radical Left, largely associated with Marxism in practice (i.e. Soviet socialism) has no working model of socialism it could point to. In this respect the radical Left seems to be in a much more vulnerable position today than it was even ten years ago (and much more so than in the 1930s). It is not easy to appreciate how, slowly but surely, the ideological 'competition' between capitalism and 'existing socialism' has been won by the former. The fear of the 'socialist alternative' was an important context in which various compromises and concessions, including the welfare state, have been made. But if 'existing socialism' has proved increasingly moribund, both materially and spiritually, then what has capitalism to fear? Even with the prospect of high unemployment and various other economic difficulties capitalism remains a creative, dynamic and libertarian society that few workers would wish to exchange for anything resembling the

Soviet model. Moreover, for the moment at least, the failure of Keynesianism and the mixed economy has given 'pure' capitalism a chance to stage a comeback as something new.

In the 1960s, it was seriously believed that the USSR and other socialist countries might catch up and surpass the West economically. This was part of the political calculus of reform in the West during Kennedy's administration in the United States. But the military question apart, the challenge of socialism has for the moment dwindled to nothingness. This is an important – indeed the essential context – against which the resurgence of neo-conservatism generally and the appeal of a return to market approach has to be understood. Yet Marxist explanation of the emergence of the new Right has not addressed this issue at all. Nor should the importance of 'existing socialism' as a bogeyman be underestimated. The proletariat has much to lose, and perhaps only chains to win, if a 'leap in the dark' leads once again to totalitarian socialism.[80] Clearly 'actually existing socialism' is largely an embarrassment to western Marxists, and nowadays fashionable theories of state capitalism provide the rationalisation for disclaiming all moral and intellectual responsibility for this type of society. Yet it is quite clear that an imaginary socialism, a Utopia based on assumptions that have been belied by history, cannot be counterposed as a serious alternative to other, real-life options.

Marxists are quick to blame the moderate Left (social democracy) for disorienting the working class in its struggle for socialism. Yet it can hardly be claimed that Marxist parties, (in Italy or France, for example) have a convincing theory of socialism or a strategy of structural or revolutionary change. Any violent confrontation with capital – such as an insurrection – seems out of question while the parliamentary road to socialism conjures up the well-worn path trodden by social democracy which leads nowhere in particular. Much was heard of 'Eurocommunism' some years ago. Yet the 'third way' (i.e. between Soviet socialism and social democracy) remains as elusive as ever, and some Marxists now find it hard to distinguish French and Italian communism from social democracy.[81]

Until about a decade ago, not only was the idea of the USSR being able to make important economic and technological advances still credible, but ideologically Maoism offered grounds for optimism to sections of the Marxist Left. Chinese socialism and Maoist versions of Marxism appeared to hold much promise, intellectually and otherwise. But if the 1970s have seen the end of affluence and a decline of the welfare state ('closing time in the gardens of the West') they have also seen the fading of Marxist hopes. May 1968 is a dim and distant memory overlaid by the usual frustrations of Mitterand-type social democracy. Maoism has been buried, as China too has had to admit that it is 'human' after all. Poland has joined Hungary and Czechoslovakia in crushing hopes of a socialism with a human face. Eurocommunism, trotted out some years ago with a great deal of fanfare, has come to nothing. Little now remains of these false dawns. True, the resurgence of intellectual Marxism, riding on the back of the explosive expansion in higher education, has led to a good deal of creativity and scholarship. But these, largely conceptual and academic exercises have yielded little that can be helpful in solving the major problems of socialist theory and practice. It is clear that as a theory of neo-imperialism and modernisation Marxism has a great deal of relevance for the Third World. But, in its present form, its relevance as a theory of social progress for western industrial societies remains doubtful. In short, a genuine socialist alternative to liberal capitalism and the welfare state, convincing both as a theory and strategy, is yet to be constituted.

4 Towards the Corporatist Welfare State: the way ahead?

The crisis of the welfare state evoked two clear radical responses, one from the Right and the other from the Left. As we saw in Chapters 2 and 3, for both these the institutional mix represented by the welfare state proves detrimental in the long run for the capitalist economy. The compromise fails to work, the contradictions prove too great. But looking at capitalist society from very diverse theoretical and normative standpoints they go on to propose very different solutions. The Right would roll back the state, at least in its welfare aspects, curtail political interference in the market economy, and rely on a self-correcting market to keep an advanced industrial economy (and society) afloat. The Left, on the other hand, points to the futility of half-way houses, to the essentially contradictory nature of capitalism, and the consequent inability of welfare capitalism either to prevent economic crises from developing or to solve them when they do occur. Add to this all the other oppressive features of capitalism and what the Marxist argument points to is the urgent need to go beyond capitalism – towards a society of free women and men making use of productive resources in a planned way for the satisfaction of needs. The solution of the Right can, at least in principle, be attempted within the confines of liberal capitalism. The solution of the Left, on the other hand, seems to involve a decisive break with capitalism. Common to both positions is a rejection of the mix, the attempted syntehsis of capitalist and socialist values, represented by the post-war welfare state. There is, however, a third option – or at least so it seems – which does not reject the mixed economy and the welfare state: this is corporatism.

Unlike the neo-conservative and Marxist perspectives, corporatism is not a major theory of society-economy relationships. Essentially, it is a pragmatic approach to the integrative problems of the political economy of advanced capitalism – – at least, that is its relevance to the present discussion. Corporatism, like many other terms in the social sciences, has been used in a variety of ways to designate the linkages between organised economic interests and the structures and processes of decision-making in the modern state. But we are not concerned here with its variety of usages and meanings.[1] And, in any case, with one or two exceptions[2] writers concerned with the analysis of the welfare state have not paid a great deal of attention to corporatism as a mode of integration and its implications for social welfare. Under these circumstances, I shall proceed by offering an ideal type of corporatism, constructed from a variety of usage and analysis most appropriate to the purposes of this study. Table 4.1 presents an ideal type of the corporatist or integrated welfare state (IWS) and contrasts it with a similar construct of the pluralist or differentiated welfare state (DWS). The contrast highlights what is most distinctive about the corporatist approach to welfare.

Table 4.1

Differentiated welfare state (DWS) * (Keynes-Beveridge)	*Integrated welfare state (IWS)* * (Post-Keynesian)
Economy – Regulation of the economy from the demand side. Government measures of 'pump priming', deficit financing, fiscal and monetary policies to stimulate or inhibit demand.	Economy – Regulation of the economy from both demand and supplyside, e.g. profits, investment, wage levels, inflation, labour market conditions. Regulation and consensus-building (with or without statutory instruments) across wide ranging economic issues.

Differentiated welfare state (DWS)* (Keynes-Beveridge)	*Integrated welfare state (IWS)** (Post-Keynesian)
Social welfare – Relatively autonomous realm seen as distinct from the economy. State provision of a range of services seen as 'socially' oriented with little explicit linkage with reference to the economy.	Social welfare – Not seen as a realm autonomous of the economy and economic policy. Interdependence and interrelationship between the social and economic recognised and institutional-ised. Functional relations and trade-offs between the economic and the social in-form policy-making.
Polity – Characterised by in-terest-group pluralism. A free-for-all or market model of the polity and societal decision-making process. Free collective bargaining in the industrial area. Pursuit of sectional interests through organised groupings, parties and parliament. Exercise of economic power without social responsibility. Parliamentary forms of government. Full civil and political liberties.	Polity – Characterised by cen-tralised pluralism. Bargain between peak associations / representatives of major economic interests over a broad range of economic and social policies. Inter-dependence of economic groups recognised and institutionalised in the form of class co-operation and social consensus. Major economic power groupings assume social responsibility. Parliamentary forms of government. Full civil and political liberties.

*The terms 'differentiation' and 'integration' are well established in social theory. As used here, the differentiated welfare state refers to the notion of a set of institutions and policies added on to the economy and polity, but seen as a relatively self-contained, delimited area set apart from them. The integrated welfare state suggests that social welfare programmes and policies are seen in relation to the economy and polity and an attempt made to integrate social welfare into the larger society.

Corporatism differs from the post-war welfare state in two respects. First and foremost it sees economic and social policy as closely interrelated and, therefore, in need of coordination. The Keynes-Beveridge approach was based on the idea of 'correcting' the tendencies of a market economy, through judicious state intervention and limited forms of social policy. The corporatist view is more synoptic: it recognises the need to harmonise the economic and the social within society as a whole. To put it another way, corporatism recognises the feedback of the social for the economic (and vice versa) and tries to come to terms with it. Thus, it sees distributive issues as inseparable from those concerning production. The upshot is that, unlike in the DWS, the economic implications of social policy are not shirked, whilst social policy objectives are introduced quite explicitly into economic policies. Second, in the corporatist approach *system* integration implicit in the institutions of the welfare state is seen as related to *social* integration.[3] In short, the functional integration between the economy and social welfare is seen as interdependent with the relations between major economic groups (i.e. capital and labour).

This implies that a productive market economy and a highly-developed system of social welfare (system integration) cannot be sustained in the long run without the co-operation and agreement of major social groupings. This 'systematic' or 'holistic' approach to problems of integration differs from the piecemeal social engineering or process approach implicit in the Keynes-Beveridge notion of the welfare state.) The owners of capital as well as producers in their organised capacity (i.e. employers' and workers' associations) are recognised as major partners in the national enterprise (*pace* Marxism, the nation is no less real an entity than class) of production and distribution, and are therefore expected to assume responsibility for making the system work. This means, for example, that, as in Austria and Sweden (see pp. 109-19) employers recognise full employment as a social objective while workers accept the need for wage moderation and higher productivity as a prerequisite for economic growth and social welfare. In contrast with the Hobbesian view of an unremitting conflict of interest in the economic as well as the political market-place and the Marxist view of a class war, the corporate view is that of society as a web of interdependent functions and interests which requires co-operation. Looking at it from another viewpoint we might say that the IWS carries the logic of collective responsibility for the social economy beyond Keynesianism. In this respect just as the welfare state (DWS) was a step forward from a largely *laiser-faire* economy and residual welfare, the IWS may be described as another step forward on the road to collective responsibility. Thus not only management of demand but also supply of productive resources, motivation for investment, and the like are issues that have to be addressed collectively.

It should be noted that the nature of state welfare does not change under corporatism. As in the DWS, it remains by and large institutional. Rather, corporatism provides an institutional framework for sustaining full employment and comprehensive social services *in the context of a liberal market society*. At the risk of repetition, it may be worth reminding ourselves that this involves, first recognising both the importance of production for distribution and the trade-off between socioeconomic phenomena, such as inflation, economic wage, social welfare and unemployment. (In this sense the IWS acknowledges the interdependence of the Keynesian and Beveridgian aspects of welfare much more clearly than the DWS.) Secondly, it recognises that in order to harmonise economic and social objectives (i.e. to maintain system integration) institutionalised co-operation between major economic interests in society becomes essential. This is the essence, for example, of the Austrian 'social partnership' between labour and capital. Admittedly, such collaboration between major organised interests involves some curtailment of a free-for-all pluralism, whether in respect of wage bargaining or social welfare. Thus what we have here is a kind of centralised pluralism which acknowledges the reality of organised economic power and its relevance for achieving social goals. No doubt the tripartite structure of decision-making – involving employers, workers and the state – implicit in corporatist problem-solving also means that the formal political order (i.e. parliament and political parties) is to some extent by-passed and thus downgraded. But this is a price –

and a somewhat ambiguous one – that has to be paid for the corporatist approach to problem-solving.[4]

By now it should be clear that in integrating the economic and social rather than treating them as warring social principles (cf. Titmuss), and in allowing a form of 'national interest' to be institutionalised beyond the level of unbridled pluralism – thus building a measure of national consensus and fiscal responsibility – the IWS goes some way towards meeting the major criticisms levelled at the welfare state, especially from the Right. Thus unprincipled government growth, overload and failure are notions that do not sit very well on the IWS. For example, Austrian incomes policy, as we shall see, is worked out *voluntarily* by the major interest groups concerned with no government control. In Sweden, too, by and large national wage bargaining has been a voluntary affair between industry and labour. This is a far cry from the government overload associated with statutory income policies, like those in Britain which have been an obvious failure. The neo-conservative critique of the welfare state (and to some extent also that of Marxists, e.g. O'Connor, regarding government failure in capitalist democracies) has tended to generalise from the Anglo-American experience. In short, it is largely a critique of the DWS. Clearly the IWS cannot escape this radical critique (directed from both the Left and the Right) entirely. Far from it. All the same it would be a serious error to underestimate the difference between pluralism and corporatism in this regard.

So far we have discussed corporatism simply in terms of the ideal-typical features of the IWS. We next look at the nature of this corporatist society, especially its political complexion, more explicitly. From the various types of corporatism distinguished by political scientists and others we may single out the distinction between liberal (democratic) and authoritarian (dictatorial) forms of corporatism as the most relevant for our purposes.[5] The former represents a *voluntary* and gradual development of corporatism, namely, the relevant attitudes and institutions, from within a pluralist society. Its essential context is the liberal capitalist society with its parliament, political parties, civil and political rights, due processes of law, and so on. This liberalism is not incompatible with certain restrictions or legal constraints, on wage agreements and strikes, for example. In fact such restrictions, especially on labour, are commonplace in the pluralist regimes of North America, and are not necessarily a feature of corporatism. The main point to be stressed is that in the IWS the liberal and voluntary framework remains firmly in place.

Authoritarian corporatism, by contrast, is involuntary. It is usually imposed, under threat of force, by a ruling elite. It involves restricting the civil and political rights of the citizen (in substance even if not always in form), curtailing or abolishing free elections, doing away with political competition between parties and parliamentary government, and above all depriving trade unions of their autonomy and integrating them forcibly into the state apparatus. Nazi Germany, Fascist Italy and Japan in the 1930s are extreme examples of this form of integration of the economic and the social sectors and of capital and labour under a (right-wing) dictatorship.[6]

From our viewpoint, *authoritarianism* really contradicts the essence of the corporatist welfare state (IWS), for the latter implies a 'social contract', i.e. *voluntary* collaboration among key socioeconomic interests who retain their freedom of action and the autonomy of their organisational base. Authoritarianism, on the other hand, presupposes the curtailment of trade union autonomy (e.g. arrest or removal of uncooperative leaders, abolition of union elections, *de facto* abolition of the right to strike, etc.) often accompanied by the restriction of civil and political rights more generally. That said, it must be recognised that liberalism and authoritarianism are matters of degree. It is useful therefore to think in terms of a continuum of liberal, authoritarian and totalitarian forms of capitalism. Clearly regimes like that of Nazi Germany come in the last category. The kind of *voluntary* co-operation among major economic groupings and the limited institutional coordination of policies *in the context of a free society* we have labelled as the IWS, belongs firmly to the liberal end of the continuum.[7]

We have outlined the DWS and the IWS as ideal types. And it is not surprising that the institutional patterns in some countries are closer to the ideal-type of the IWS than in others. Elements of a corporatist approach have been present in a number of European countries for quite some time. It would be useful, therefore, to look at their experience and to see what conclusions might be drawn from it.

Let me point out at the very outset that none of the English-speaking countries can be said to have moved far towards the IWS. They have remained essentially DWSs and in at least one – the USA – even the structure and ideology of the welfare state is not established very firmly. Britain has been flirting with corporatist forms since about the mid-1960s without ever achieving a viable national consensus in favour of such an approach. Recent British history is littered with national plans, incomes policies (voluntary as well as statutory), a social contract and so on; in short, fragments of corporatism introduced *ad hoc* and often as a temporary expedient.[8] As an OECD study points out, this is a far cry from the relatively enduring social consensus developed by countries like Austria and, to a lesser extent, Sweden which embrace a notion of social management much wider than an incomes policy.[9] Britain's perfunctory experiments with corporatism and their failure (*pace* the social contract of 1976-9 between the Labour government and the trade union movement which is the closest Britain seems to have come to a relatively coherent, comprehensive and successful – at least for a time – attempt in this direction) have a significance that goes well beyond the British Isles.

As the leading DWS in the English-speaking world, post-war Britain served as a model of the welfare state and its achievements. Since the mid-1960s, however, an ailing economy, relative decline in social expenditure compared with other countries and, not least, the failure to establish viable forms of corporatism have left a depressing legacy of lame-duck welfarism and half-baked interventionism. Increasingly, therefore Britain has come to represent a negative experience, both in respect of the DWS and the viability of an IWS, and as a result the English-speaking world has lacked a positive model of welfare capitalism. It is partly for this reason that monetarist and market solutions have acquired so much credibility in so short a time on both sides of the Atlantic. In English-speaking countries we have had very little acquaintance and virtually no experience of a corporatist welfare state.

It is primarily certain European countries, above all Austria, but also Sweden, West Germany and the Netherlands among others, that offer us the experience – more or less successful, more or less stable – of corporatism.[10] The latter is a form of collectivism that is far from 'reluctant', and it is not surprising that it is in countries with a developed social democratic and labour movement that corporatism has been able to develop most fully. Conversely, countries in which the labour movement is weak and there is no social democratic politics, notably the USA, have been the furthest from the corporatist path. As Robert Salisbury writes: 'the political strength of business in America and the concomitant weakness of labour may well help us understand why it has only been in times of severe crisis that both sides have been willing to sit together.'[11] On the other hand, countries with a large Communist Party (e.g. Italy and France) have also failed to develop corporatist institutions. In the former, given the weakness of labour, reliance has been placed on the market forces to correct the economy, with social objectives taking a second place. In the latter, given the anti-capitalist thrust of communist-dominated labour movements, class collaboration has not been a viable proposition for either labour or capital. Perhaps Berlinguer's 'historic compromise' (collaboration between Christian Democrats and the Communists for the sake of stability and progress) might have brought Italy closer to an experiment in corporatism, but in the event it failed to materialise.[12] However, the conditions which favour the emergence of corporatism, though an important issue, would not be our concern here (see, however, p. 174 below). What I should like to outline now is the nature and experience of corporatism in Austria and briefly Sweden. This will serve to illustrate the arguments presented above in favour of corporatism.

Austria

Among western industrial countries post-war Austria comes closest to the model of an IWS. And it is no coincidence that Austria's record on economic growth, full employment, social welfare expenditure and industrial peace in the post-war years has been exceptionally good.[13] Its recent performance is particularly impressive. In the 1970s when one western country after another succumbed to economic stagnation, double-figure inflation, rising unemployment, industrial conflicts and cutbacks in social expenditure, Austria managed to maintain an enviably good record on virtually all of these.[14] And most commentators agree that a major, if not *the* major, reason for Austria's resilience in coping with the economic crisis of the 1970s is its institution of 'social partnership' – in short, corporatism.[15]

A number of historical and geopolitical factors seem to have contributed to the emergence of the peculiarly Austrian way of achieving consensus on economic and social policies, institutionalised in the form of the social partnership. The traumatic experience of the inter-war years involving acute social conflict, civil war and the collapse of democratic institutions; international status as an alliance-free *Kleinstaat* between East and West pursuing an independent course; the strength of labour and social democracy; the somewhat weak position of private capital as shown by the fact that public, co-operative and other forms of social enterprise account for one-third of the whole economy – these are some of the main factors that help us understand the emergence and success of Ausrian corporatist developments.[16]

The essence of the Austrian social partnership is the *voluntary* co-operation between the two major interests, capital and labour, over wide ranging economic issues. The post-war objective of achieving economic and social stability led to the setting-up of the Joint Commission for Wage and Price Questions in 1957. The Joint Commission is one of the most important institutions of the social partnership, but has no legal foundation as such. Four economic partner organisations are responsible for running it. Between them they cover agriculture, industry and labour. The Joint Commission has three sub-committees concerned with wages, prices and economic and social questions, respectively. Government representatives attend the Commission's meetings, but have no voting rights. In any case, the Commission is not so much a forum for the representation of interests as a corporate body which seeks to arrive at a consensus and makes unanimous decisions. This is certainly the case with the two major decision-making bodies – the wages and the prices sub-committees. The principle of unanimity and consensus means that any one of the four constituent associations can bring the autonomous partnership to a halt.

The full Joint Commission meets monthly with the Federal Chancellor as Chairman. The full assembly of the Commission also meets quarterly as an 'economic policy forum' with the national Bank, Finance Ministry and specialists drawn from the constituent associations taking part. It is however the Chairmen's Discussion, which takes place before each full meeting of the Joint Commission, that is of key importance. Here the chairmen of the four associations work out and agree on compromise solutions. Decisions not already taken in the sub-committees are arrived at here. The final decision of the full Commission is then simply a formality.

It should be noted that the decisions of the Joint Commission have no legal status and must be granted statutory authority by the state. Wage policies and recommendations are however autonomous and have no legal standing. Wage and salary negotiations are conducted by the respective unions in each industry and wage moderation is less a function of centrally-established guidelines than that of a climate of opinion created by the social partnership and other consensus-making bodies. As regards statutory endorsement of social partners' decisions it is virtually 'unthinkable' that parliament could do otherwise. In fact, the practice of the so-called 'twofold parity' ensures an interlock between political parties, the social partners and the parliament. The top officials involved in social partnership are usually also Members of Parliament and functionaries of their own parties.[17]

The social partnership is based on the recognition that consensus among major economic groupings – chiefly employers and workers – is a prerequisite for the smooth functioning of a modern industrial market economy. In particular it is recognised that if social policy aims (e.g. full employment and social welfare) are to be achieved then economic policy issues must be addressed. More generally, the interdependence of the economic and the social is acknowledged and the relationship, including the trade-off between economic wage and social welfare, wage levels and inflation, inflation and unemployment forms the basis of the general policy approach. Thus ideological billing and rhetoric apart, Austrian political parties and economic groups agree on the objectives of economic growth, full employment and social protection as well as those of economic and political stability. The social partnership quite apart from its contribution to economic stability and growth, is also an important political stabiliser. For, irrespective of which of the two major parties are in power, both capital and labour (each closely affiliated to one or the other) have a permanent voice in an important area of national decision-making. Moreover, the principle of 'twofold parity' ensures that each side has equal representation.[18]

In brief, what we have here is a form of *permanent* incomes and prices policy, voluntarily arrived at by the major economic interests and closely related to a set of agreed national objectives, full employment and economic growth, to name the two most important ones. It is important to distinguish the Austrian system of corporate decision-making based on consensus, with prices and incomes policy forming part of a wider notion of collective responsibility, from the *ad hoc* and temporary forms of incomes policies instituted (e.g. in Britain) to deal with a crisis situation. Stop-gap incomes policies, as Britain's experience shows, give rise to what has been called the 're-entry problem' – the return to free collective bargaining, sometimes wreaking havoc on the economy in the process. It is the long-term and voluntary nature of Austrian social partnership, with its firm commitment to the idea of concord and to the principle of unanimous decision-making, that distinguishes the corporatist Austrian welfare state from say, the British welfare state.

Britain remains essentially a pluralist order in which limited forms of incomes policies represent a temporary suspension of the norm of free collective bargaining. Moreover, in the absence of a national consensus, government attempts at curbing wage militancy and freedom of action on the shop-floor through legislative restrictions appear as an imposition from above. It is scarcely surprising that they fail in the long run. True, Labour government's social contract with the trade unions, both in its comprehensiveness and its explicit recognition of the interdependence of economic and social policies, was probably the closest approximation in Britain to a corporatist approach to welfare. But it did not have the support and general assent of either the employers or the opposition party. It was instituted to deal with a crisis – hyperinflation, rising unemployment and a stagnant economy – and in this sense was regarded, at any rate by the workers, as a temporary measure. While it succeeded in restraining wages and bringing down inflation, the hoped-for economic recovery failed to arrive. After three years of restraint, the pent up demand for higher wages erupted in the winter of 1979 burying the social contract as well as its achievements in the process. British attempts at 'instrumental' forms of corporatism, not rooted in a national consensus and therefore doomed to be temporary expedients, are a far cry from the relatively enduring institutions and ideology of the Austrian welfare state.

It should be noted that one of the assumptions underlying national consensus and social partnership in Austria is that the relative shares of capital and labour in the national income are not to be disturbed. The ratio scale between wages and profits is apparently well established and what is emphasised is the need to make the 'pie' bigger rather than redistribute income.[19] In this sense it is clear that the IWS is not a socialist institution. Its structures are firmly embedded in a market economy which relies on profits and must remain competitive internationally. But *en revanche* the Austrian welfare state, as compared with a DWS such as Britain, seems less likely to foster the illusion of being redistributive and socialistic. It could be that the free-for-all of a DWS is in one sense to labour's advantage. Thanks to the security provided by full employment and social benefits labour can increase its share relative to capital through free collective bargaining. But it is also clear that such a tactic can only work in the short run. In the long run, decline in productivity and profits result in declining economic growth, which in turn leads to unemployment and cuts in social programmes. This is roughly what seems to have happened in Britain.

Put another way, the IWS takes a *dynamic* and *societal*, view of the relation between the market economy, full employment and state welfare programmes. It is as though the wider implications of Keynesianism are grasped from the beginning and the necessary institutions and attitudes developed to sustain welfare capitalism. The IWS thus emerges as the appropriate framework within which to accommodate the logic of a Keynesian mixed economy. This is evident in Austria's success in maintaining full employment, low rates of inflation, economic growth and an exceptionally low level of industrial conflict into the 1980s. For example, in 1980 the rate of unemployment in Austria was 1·9 per cent compared with 6·8 per cent in UK; the rate of price inflation for the 1970s averaged at 6·3 per cent, less than half of UK's 13·6 per cent; whilst the strike minutes per employee averaged a mere 5 compared with UK's 274.

After the first oil price explosion, Austria adopted counter-cyclical policies – financial, economic and related to employ-ment – to combat the growing recession. Large deficits in the budget and in the balance of payments were accepted in order to maintain full employment. This policy was feasible largely because the social partnership – through wage and price moderation – could keep inflation in check. As an OECD report comments, 'the incomes policy encompassed by the social partnership has played a key role in maintaining good cost and price trends... with inflation under control, the authorities have been able to pursue a more expansionary fiscal policy than would otherwise have been the case.'[20] Naturally, Austria has not retrenched social expenditure but has decided to reduce the budget deficit recently. This is to be done in part through slightly reduced public expenditure and in part through higher social security taxes.

While Austria is no socialist haven – for example, income inequalities have remained stable over the years – it is also clear that through corporatist arrangements Austria has prevented the costs of capitalist market dislocations 'to lie where they fall'. Instead of resorting to a free-for-all, in which fractions of labour or capital win a skirmish temporarily but whose un-intended consequences are high inflation, unemployment and the retrenchment of social programmes, Austria has main-tained intact through the 1970s – on all accounts a difficult decade for capitalism as well as welfare – Keynesian welfare capitalism. The Austrian experience would thus seem to chal-lenge the arguments advanced by neo-conservatives as well as by Marxists about the incompatibility of welfare with capitalism. Rather it suggests that the dysfunctions of welfare seized upon by these critics have to do, primarily, with the DWSs of the English-speaking world.

It could, however, be argued as Marxists do, that given the international nature of the current crisis corporatism too can only stave off its effects temporarily. It is only a matter of time before corporatism comes apart in the face of the contradictions of capitalism. In a slightly different form the same point is made by many non-Marxist commentators, who argue that with continuing economic stagnation it will become increasingly difficult, if not impossible, to maintain the essentials of social partnership in Austria; that whilst the social partnership can weather short lived crises and recessions as it has in the past, it cannot survive a long period of stagnation which takes economic growth, an essential precondition for social consensus, out of the equation. It has also been claimed that the Austrian economy reaped the advantage of certain special conditions in the post-war decades. These are now disappearing making the economy much more open to international competition. In these circumstances major structural adjustments would be necessary resulting in unemployment and social tension. These are likely to strain the system to the utmost. Further, current policies of maintaining 'social' full employment would make the problems of raising productivity and adjusting to new conditions more difficult.[21] Undoubtedly there is some truth in these observations; their pertinence and plausibility can hardly be questioned. But no social system, including the IWS, can be immune from the 'creative gales of destruction' to which modern market economies must give rise. At least the IWSs like Austria can point to a good record, so far, of system maintenance which suggests that they can adapt to new conditions with greater equity and justice than any other form of capitalism.

Sweden

Sweden may be said to lie between Austria, with its well-developed and comprehensive form of corporatism, on the one hand and pluralist states, such as Britain, on the other. Further-more, in many other ways Sweden's approach to social questions differs from Austria's, in the pursuit of equality, of worker's control of industry and the like. But these differences need not concern us here.

In Sweden the connection between economic and social policies was appreciated as early as the 1930s when the Social Democratic government put a form of Keynesian employment policy into effect. In this connection the Labour Market Board (LMB) was set up in order to keep the economic infrastructure in line with the broader social objectives of full employment, economic growth, egalitarian ('solidaristic') wage structure, and a high level of social welfare. In the post-war years the LMB has become established as a major pillar of the Swedish welfare state.[22] Among its major functions is counter-cyclical investment planning – through a series of incentives and con-trols firms are encouraged to set aside profits as reserve funds to be invested in times of recession. A second major function is labour market planning – through a series of measures (e.g. retraining and help with relocation,) labour is encouraged to be mobile occupationally, industrially and geographically. These measures, very extensive in nature, help maintain em-ployment (e.g. through counter-cyclical investment) and promote economic growth (e.g. through higher labour mobil-ity and greater efficiency resulting from retraining).

An important feature of wages policy in Sweden has been the unions' attempt to obtain equal pay for equal work ('wage solidarity') irrespective of the profits of particular firms or industries. This has meant accepting that declining industries and less profitable firms must be allowed to run down and the labour released as a result redeployed in growing and profit-able sectors of the economy. Swedish trade unions have based their strategy on the recognition that the social objectives of full employment, generous welfare provision and wage solidarity are interdependent with economic growth and industrial modernisation.[23] Here the contrast with Britain is telling. British unions, unlike the Swedish, have clung to restrictive practices and over-manning, refusing, on the whole, any responsibility for modernisation and higher productivity. This has paved the way for Thatcherism – ostensibly a drastic measure to 'save' the economy and the nation from bank-ruptcy – with its aggressive policy of disemployment, forced wage moderation and cuts in the social services.

The Swedish LMB, though formally a tripartite body, is in effect bipartite. Government is present but the major partners are the workers' and employers' organisations, and the insti-tutionalised co-operation between employers' and workers' representatives has played an important part in helping secure consensus over broad economic and social objectives.[24] A more specific, but crucial, area of social co-operation has been the annual wage bargaining at the national level – a process of bargaining between employers and workers without any governmental participation. This wage bargaining is based on a carefully calculated estimate of the increase in the national product. A broad framework of agreement outlining the prin-ciple of wage settlement is arrived at by the SAF for the employers and the LO for the workers.[25] Individual industry agreements are then negotiated by the two sides within the framework laid down at the national level. Undoubtedly, this involves a good deal of centralisation in wage negotiations and agreements. For example, the industry agreements are treated as provisional until approved by the executive boards of the SAF and LO. The agreements then become mandatory and the law can be used to uphold agreements. In addition the LO, the central federation, keeps a firm control over its constituent unions. Despite this centralisation however the Swedish economy has had a good deal of 'wage drift'.[26]

Overall, the Swedish approach to wage negotiations shows an appreciation of two things: the importance of wage moder-ation in conditions of full employment and the inter-dependence of social and economic policies generally. As a result such questions as wages, wage solidarity and social welfare are considered in relation to broader economic issues, notably that of production. In this way Sweden seems to be upholding the major tenets of corporatism (see Table 4.1).

Until the mid-1970s Sweden's record on economic growth, inflation and social welfare was, on the whole, exceptionally good, so much so that it came to be seen as the 'model' welfare state of the post-war years. During the second half of the 1970s, however, Sweden has run into some difficulties.[27] International competitiveness has suffered, productivity has remained low and industrial production has stagnated. Full employment (or something close to it) has been maintained but, it appears, at the cost of heavy government subsidy to industry. This is likely to slow down, if not actually impede, structural adjustment to changing economic conditions. Public expenditure and budget deficits are at an all-time high while marginal rates of taxation are the highest among OECD nations.[28] The LMB operations, as well as annual wage bargaining, the two main props of Sweden's social consensus and prosperity, though well-adapted to the buoyant conditions of post-war western economy have not not been able to cope with the prolonged international recession of the 1970s. In retrospect it appears that the 'social' has been over-emphasised at the cost of the 'economic' – full employment, good wages and social welfare in preference to profitability and labour 'shake out'. The Swedish authorities are now being obliged to make some of the necessary adjustments. In part the difficulty stems from the reflationary and socially-oriented policies followed by the government to counter the recession following the first oil crisis. These policies were based on the expectation that the economic recession, like the others that had preceded it in the post-war decades, would be short lived and 'normal' conditions would return soon. These expectations, needless to add, have not been fulfilled.[29]

True, Sweden has not been as successful as the more thoroughly corporatist Austria, but it would be unwise to claim too much for corporatism as such. Clearly other factors are involved and in part account for the different situation in which the two countries find themselves. None the less, it should be noted that Sweden has managed to come through the recession with very little social strife and with the Keynesian welfare state, built up under the long reign of the Social Democratic government, largely intact. Moreover, recent changes in policy which include moderate wage settlement, some easing of social expenditure and lower marginal tax rates suggest that Swedish welfare capitalism has the flexibility to cope with economic problems of the 1980s. It is also not without significance that the Social Democratic Party, voted out of office in 1976 after forty-four years in government, was returned to power in late 1982 on a platform committed, *inter alia*, to maintaining if not extending social expenditure and other elements of the welfare state.[30]

Concluding Remarks

In sum both Austria and Sweden, albeit in varying degrees and forms, have built into their political economy the basic elements of the IWS. The integration of the economic and social, the concern with supply side economics (e.g. with labour mobility and productivity) in addition to the management of demand, centralised 'social partnership' between capital and labour are some of these. Available evidence suggests that thanks to corporatist features these countries have thus far been able to accommodate the dynamics of Keynesian welfare capitalism relatively well.

Undoubtedly the current economic recession, which began in the 1970s and whose typical as well as novel features may be described as 'stagflation', has posed serious problems even for these corporatist democracies. Moreover, questions about the viability and limitations of corporatism have been raised on other grounds. In chapter 6 we shall consider some of these criticisms briefly. But there is at least one issue which should be addressed at this stage. Put simply, it is this. Corporatism is a form of *national* response to a range of problems presented by welfare capitalism. Yet on all accounts the current crisis is that of capitalism as an *international* phenomenon. The corporatist approach may therefore be of little help in resolving those international problems connected, for example, with trade, exchange rates, the multinationals and relations with the Third World. This is an important point and certainly draws attention to the limits of corporatism. The post-war prosperity of capitalism was made possible by a set of international agreements which provided a framework for monetary stability and free trade.[31] It appears as if the reconstruction of a new international framework may, once again, be a necessary condition for stability and growth in capitalist countries. No doubt this issue must be addressed at the supra-national level. Other issues, including alternative sources of energy, also seem to require a transnational approach.

These conditions do not, however, diminish the relevance of corporatism as far as the internal situation is concerned. For while capitalist countries try to find an international solution to the crisis they have to live (i.e. produce and distribute) largely as nation-states. Corporatism therefore remains relevant in the attempt *to cope nationally* with the effects of a crisis which is undoubtedly international in nature. Secondly, even when international agreement is reached and some of the deeper, underlying causes of the crisis removed much of economic life would go on within the confines of the nation-state and, presumably, in a context (e.g. the 'collapse of work') that might need close co-operation between major socio-economic interests. On this score too an integrated approach to welfare would retain its relevance.

For the moment, therefore, I should like to offer the following by way of conclusion. It appears that a global approach, a sort of societal policy which is based more or less explicitly on voluntary class co-operation and which recognises that the social and the economic are two sides of the same coin, offers a better chance of maintaining the essentials of the post-war welfare state. At the very least, then, corporatism seems well suited to harmonise within a national framework – a market economy, a liberal democracy, full employment and a system of social welfare aimed at ensuring a decent minimum standard of living for all.

5 Social Reform and Welfare: the Social Democratic response

In this chapter we consider the response of the Liberal/Social Democratic 'Centre' or 'Centre-Left' – the political and intellectual position most closely associated with the post-war welfare state – to the current crisis in welfare. Compared with the Right and the radical Left, the Centre-Left tends to be much more eclectic and diffuse doctrinally. It represents essentially a pragmatic and practical, rather than a theoretically rigorous and systematic tradition. In this tradition I include Fabian socialists (e.g. Titmuss) interested in the pursuit of equality through social policy as well as moderate collectivists (e.g. Beveridge) concerned with using the state welfare services to guarantee a basic minimum. Their approach to collectivism and welfare differs more in degree than in kind. Both groups have a commitment to the welfare state and to political democracy and freedom. Both employ a strategy of reform from above and rely on professionals and state administrators to put enlightened social policies into effect.

A convenient British label for this genre of reformism is 'Fabianism' and will be used in this chapter more or less interchangeably with 'social democratic' to indicate this Centre-Left position. Although the term Fabianism is not directly transferrable to countries outside Britain, including the United States, the assumption made here is that in almost all western industrial countries intellectual and political orientations akin to it can be identified. In Britain social scientists such as Richard Titmuss, T. H. Marshall and Peter Townsend represent this genre of thinking and collectivist

121

approach. True, they (and others discussed below) differ in many important ways in their thinking. Many, moreover, might not wish to wear the label 'Fabian' or 'social democrat'. Be that as it may, the main point is that the reformist tradition of enhancing social welfare through pragmatic state intervention is seen here as a distinctive approach, paralleling the neo-conservative, Marxist and the corporatist views outlined already. Finally, it should be pointed out that we are not here concerned with liberal or social democratic approaches from a party political standpoint, which may not only differ from country to country but in some cases might be quite close to the corporatist position outlined in the previous chapter. Here our main concern is with the intellectual standpoint largely associated with the post-war welfare state (DWS) (see Chapter 4).

The impasse in which the Keynesian managed economy found itself from about the mid-1970s and the resulting implications for social welfare have left the Fabians in a quandary. As Donnison points out, post-war Fabian thinking about social policy took economic growth (and we might add full employment) for granted. Social policy was therefore seen as 'dealing with the *redistribution* of the fruits of economic growth, the management of its human effects, and the compensation of those who suffered from them.'[1] There was little concern with the *productive* aspects of welfare capitalism. This did not seem unreasonable in the 1950s and 1960s when by all accounts it looked as if the pre-war problem of economic recessions had finally been solved.

But once capitalist economy was confronted with stagflation, and Keynesian recipes proved ineffectual to overcome it, the situation changed radically. As growth and full employment ceased to be valid assumptions, the argument for higher social expenditure and redistribution began to look increasingly unrealistic. In any case rising unemployment was a cruel reminder of the importance of 'economic welfare', which could no longer be guaranteed by the welfare state. In Britain, Thatcherism capitalised on the hiatus between Labourite stress on distributive collectivism, and the sorry state of the British economy and its productive base. Thatcherites emphasised their own 'realistic' appraisal of the needs and priorities of the British economy, contrasting it with the 'mindless' collectivism and the economically disastrous growth of social expenditure favoured by the Fabians.[2] In the United States Reagan politics capitalised on a similar disjunction between the nation's apparent desire for higher consumption (both private and public) as well as lower taxes on the one hand and the precarious state of the economy on the other.[3] By and large, in English-speaking countries, the policy initiative has been seized by the Right while social democracy finds itself in disarray.

The Absence of Theory

But where does this leave the Fabian Centre – the main intellectual support of the post-war welfare state? What has been its response to the 'crisis' so far? Perhaps the most revealing thing about the Fabian response is that it is virtually a non-response. What Rustin has noted recently *à propos* Britain has wider validity; namely, that the Centre seems to have collapsed without a fight in the face of political and intellectual onslaught of the new Right. Rustin believes that the radical Left must take some of the blame for this. He writes, the 'discrediting of welfare reformism, and the failure to maintain much belief in its further potential, has surely helped to clear the way for the attack on it from the Right.'[4]

Rustin's point is well taken. But quite apart from the peculiarities of the British situation, he fails to address the more fundamental issues involved. There are two. First, the key role of Keynesian economics in underpinning the mixed economy, which in turn formed the mainstay of the social welfare services. It is not so much the attack on reformism by the radical Left (which could largely be ignored by Fabians and others as long as the 'going was good') as the increasing difficulty of the mixed economy and the crumbling of its intellectual prop, namely Keynesianism, that has silenced the Centre. What recent events have also underlined is the extent to which social democratic reformism and strategy of change depended on the smooth functioning of the mixed economy. Moreover, this is a point that social Fabians such as Titmuss and Townsend not only did not come to terms with but scarcely acknowledged. Successful economic management and growth were taken for granted. The market economy, there-fore, tended to be seen either as an engine of inequality and privilege, or else ignored as irrelevant to the moral case for egalitarianism and social justice. In any case the arguments centred largely on distribution and collective consumption. But once the economy moved into a no-growth situation public attention shifted towards the problems of production, inflation and the like. Moreover the distributive struggle (espe-cially that centred on economic wage) became so intensive as to threaten the very conditions of production (hyperinflation, reduced profits, bankruptcies, etc.). The situation in which value conflict over distribution could be waged around social expenditure in a civilised sort of way vanished robbing the Centre of much of its appeal. The Centre has been rather more vulnerable in Britain in part because the country's steady economic decline is associated with the post-war period of welfare consensus and also because by the end of the 1970s the economy was really in bad shape.

The second and more basic point to be made from the perspective of this book is that Fabianism lacks an articulated theory (both normative and positive) of the welfare state. Indeed, as already pointed out, its approach to social reform has been piecemeal and pragmatic, based on a range of economic, political and social assumptions which have not been made explicit, and with little recourse to theory. More-over, a similar lack of fundamental thinking about social democracy more generally has been characteristic of the 1960s and the 1970s. Perhaps the last (the only?) systematic statement of the theoretical standpoint of post-war social democracy came from Anthony Crosland.[5] Recent years have seen a spate of books about social democracy and socialism but lack the elegance, verve and weight of his influential treatise.[6] Through-out the 1960s and for a good part of the 1970s both welfare statism and parliamentary socialism have relied on a mix of technocratic and moral arguments (e.g. *ad hoc* statements in favour of welfare).[7] It is hardly surprising that the Centre which intellectually speaking never really had much coherence and weight should 'collapse' as problems began to mount for which neither Keynesianism nor a roused social conscience had any solution.

The atheoretical tradition dominant in the study of social welfare, the empirical study of discrete social problems and their solution through administrative reforms, has often been noted.[8] Yet it would be wrong to suggest that thirty years of welfare statism and the study of social problems has failed to generate any theory whatsoever. But this theory is largely concerned with what might be called social problems located *within* the framework and practice of the welfare state. Social research and theorising have often been of an applied kind concerned with poverty, stigma, selectivity, universality, and territorial justice. In this approach – and this is the nub of the matter from the viewpoint of the current crisis – there has been very little concern with trying to understand the welfare state as a whole, as a *social system*. The focus has been almost entirely on social policy and administration, whilst the wider social-structural context of state welfare activity has been ignored.

Writing recently Robson, a veteran British Fabian, bemoans the absence of a clear rationale of the welfare state – a theory or vision that would both elicit *moral* support from the people and act as a guide to policy-makers. 'There is at present no philosophy of the welfare state', writes Robson, 'and there is an urgent and deep need for such a theory.'[9] For Robson, the welfare state cannot simply be an instrument for distributing and allocating resources through collectivist channels. If it were to be merely that then it would become an extension of the capitalist market-place, an arena for grabbing what different groups can by exerting pressure on the government rather than a system which serves the community as a whole in accordance with nationally-based priorities. The latter, however, presupposes a welfare *society* which, in turn, demands a measure of national consensus or unity. This unity was present in Britain after the war, but Robson finds little evidence of it in the 1970s. The result is a void. The welfare state is not based on a broadly accepted altruism grounded in a social philosophy: 'Political scientists have not provided a theory of the proper province of state action in the contemporary world ... The term welfare state offers no guide to the proper limits of individual freedom or governmental action.'[10] Robson, moreover, raises the question of duties or obligations (corresponding to rights) within the welfare state. For example, given the interrelationship between the economic and social sectors of society does free collective bargaining by workers, professionals and others, aimed at maximising sectional interest, make sense? Robson believes that maximising self-interest in this way is more 'appropriate to a *laisser-faire* state'. It is scarcely 'compatible with a welfare society', for 'in such a society welfare is not only something created by the state through the action of public authorities, but is also generated by the actions and attitudes of individuals, groups and institutions.'[11] In fact, Robson seems to be drawing attention, *inter alia*, to the weaknesses of a plural welfare state (DWS) and some of the issues he raises, for example the need for restraint and for consensus over national goals and priorities, point towards a corporatist solution (IWS). But it is not a solution that Robson consciously looks at.

Robson's book is important because of the questions it asks rather than the answers it provides. It is one of the rare attempts by a British Fabian to look at the welfare state as a whole, critically, and as a social system linked with other institutional aspects of the society of which it is a part. Robson's principal thesis is that 'we are vainly trying to have a welfare state without having achieved a welfare society'.[12] i.e. without generating those attitudes and outlook necessary to sustain the ideal of a welfare state. Despite important differences in method and objectives, Robson's work is comparable to Janowitz's elegant sociological study of the crisis of the welfare state in the US.[13]

Others, notably Bell in the USA and Hirsch on the other side of the Atlantic, have also raised the question of an adequate theory, normative and positive, of the welfare state. These writers believe that piecemeal social engineering and *ad hoc* collectivism are not enough. Without the necessary intellectual and moral underpinning, the welfare state far from being integrative, becomes anomic. Bell notes that while the state's role in managing economic and social affairs has grown enormously there is neither an adequate sociology nor social philosophy of the 'public household' (i.e. government revenue and expenditure). Meanwhile the combination of a market economy, a democratic polity and a growing public sector is proving fatal. For Bell, contemporary economic dilemmas

confronting Western societies derive from the fact that we have sought to combine bourgeois appetites which resist curbs on acquisitiveness, either morally or by taxation; a democratic polity which, increasingly and understandably, demands more and more social services as entitlements; and an individualist ethos which at best defends the idea of personal liberty, and at worst evades the necessary social responsibilities and social sacrifices which a communal society demands. In sum we have had no normative commitment to a public household or a public philosophy that would mediate private conflicts.[14]

The upshot is that the public household 'is not a community but an arena, in which there are no normative rules (other than bargaining) to define the common good and adjudicate conflicting claims on the basis of rights.'[15] Bell, in the manner of a latterday Durkheim, looks for 'some transcendent tie' that would bind individuals in a society 'sufficiently for them to make, when necessary, the necessary sacrifices of self-interest.'[16]

In the course of a novel and elegant thesis on the social limits to growth, Hirsch poses a similar problem.[17] The growing collective regulation of the economy and public provision of goods and services is, none the less, taking place in the context of individualism and the pursuit of self-interest. Without a social ethic that would legitimise existing regulations and distributive patterns the public sector tends to be less a community and more an arena concerned, like the private or market sector, with egotistical and sectional interests. Hence in the public sphere technical manipulation alone is no longer effective. For in the absence of the appropriate motives and attitudes on the part of the actors (restraint, acceptance of a social ethic) technical measures, (e.g. those aimed at inflation) do not work. Rather pessimistically for the liberal capitalist society, Hirsch concludes that we 'may be near the limit of explicit social organization possible without a supporting social morality. Additional correctives in its absence simply do not take.'[18]

The absence of a macro-theory of the welfare state is, in one sense, an indictment of post-war Fabian thinking about welfare which has tended to neglect, if not altogether avoid, the systematic analysis of the welfare state as a social structure. The empiricist, practical and largely atheoretical approach prevalent in the study of social welfare has been noted already. However, at least two post-war social scientists, Titmuss and Marshall, who have made outstanding contributions to the analysis of welfare, merit attention. How far is their work relevant to the development of a theory of the welfare state? We begin with Titmuss.

It is no secret that Titmuss, though outstandingly original and incisive in his analyses, was not a systematic thinker. In fact he had little patience with theorising and did not even care much for a schematic approach to the study of welfare. His was a critical intelligence which illuminated specific issues in social policy supremely well, but never sought to comprehend the 'welfare state' as a macro-social system. He never explored its relationship with the rest of the society systematically whether at the level of values or functions. 'Titmuss was not a theorist... He was suspicious of attempts to construct broad, general theories of social policy development or the roles and functions of social services.'[19] It is a pity that this was so, for more than anyone else working within the academic tradition of social administration, Titmuss took a wide, societal view of social welfare. His account of the development of social policy in Britain during the war years, the study of income distribution and social change, the Fabian lecture on the 'irresponsible' society, and above all the idea of social welfare as an expression of social solidarity and community all attest to his interest and insight into the society-welfare relationship.[20]

Unfortunately there is too much in Titmuss's writing that is *ad hoc*, improvised and eclectic, and too little that is worked out systematically to be able to provide the foundations of a theory of the welfare state. Much of his work was a polemic against the ideology and practice of economic *laisser-faire*. In the economic climate of the 1950s and 1960s his defence of the 'institutional' approach against the 'residual' was an important contribution to the debate then taking place around policy issues. Titmuss had the good fortune (or misfortune) not to see the end of the Indian summer of the Keynesian mixed economy and the welfare state. How he would have responded to the intellectual challenge to Fabianism posed by the political economy of stagflation can only be guessed at.

Unlike Titmuss, Marshall is primarily a theoretical sociologist interested in the social analysis of the welfare state. His concerns are academic and analytical rather than practical and reformist. Among social democratic thinkers, Marshall is virtually unique in his attempt to analyse the welfare state as a social system, especially in relation to capitalism. He sees the welfare state largely as the institutionalisation of social rights in a capitalist society.[21] It is a part of the development of the idea and institutions of citizenship – encompassing civil, political and social rights – in western democratic societies. In this sense capitalism, democracy and state welfare institutions form a part of the evolutionary development of the West. None the less Marshall, somewhat like Titmuss, also notes the conflict of values inherent in a social system comprising a market economy, a democratic polity and a state welfare sector. For instance there is the problem of reconciling the value of inequality inherent in the market with the egalitarianism implicit in the idea of meeting needs. But whereas for Titmuss the values underlying the economic and the social sectors – capitalist market economy and social welfare – are diametrically opposed, for Marshall they are not so. Rather the problem is one of achieving a judicious mix of values. The copresence of differing values and principles within a social structure is not necessarily a source of weakness. In fact it could be the opposite. Marshall believes that if the respective spheres of the market economy, the polity and the welfare system are clearly demarcated and respected, no major problems need arise.[22]

We may point out that this presupposes a good measure of social consensus and discipline concerning the nature and functioning of social institutions. It is more likely to be achieved in the corporatist rather than the plural welfare state. In any case Marshall fails to address the problem of how, given the sociopolitical dynamics of a pressure group polity and the competitive ethos of the economic and political market-place, a neat division of labour between the various sectors of society could be maintained? Yet in recent writings Marshall reiterates

129

the view that current difficulties are largely due to the confusion between the respective role of the market and welfare sectors.[23] These writings also reveal Marshall as a 'moderate' collectivist, one who subscribes, more or less, to the Beveridgian concept of welfare based on the idea of a 'national minimum' available as of right.[24] For Marshall, that principle provided a clear rationale for the scope of state action but postwar developments have led away from it. We shall return to this point.

Marshall's approach has the merit of looking at the welfare state (a) in a systematic rather than an *ad hoc* and empirical manner, and (b) in relation to its wider social context. But it too suffers from some of the limitations associated with Fabianism. First, it centres largely on *values* and *value conflicts* within welfare capitalism and ignores the *functional* relationships involved between different parts of the social structure of democratic-welfare-capitalism. Thus Marshall maintains that value pluralism might be beneficial, or at least need not be detrimental, to the social structure. Yet the issues raised by Robson, Bell and Hirsch, for example, throw serious doubt on this proposition. And quite apart from that, institutions are not simply *value realms* but also *material entities* that are interrelated and interdependent. 'Dysfunctional' relations could therefore develop between them (e.g. abolition of poverty could seriously affect the work ethic and the profitability of industry) resulting in a loss of effectiveness overall.[25] Unless the welfare sector is so modest and small as not to interfere with the market economy, and the major political parties agree to maintain such a stable system, it is difficult to see how a balance between the economic, political and welfare elements of the social structure could be maintained.

As we have seen in earlier chapters, current problems of the welfare state seem to have a lot to do with dysfunctions arising out of the relationship between the various sectors of democratic welfare capitalism. The Marshallian approach does not come to grips with this problem. Nor does it point out the basis on which a consensus about the respective role of state welfare, market economy, party politics and the like (Marshall's mix of values underlying the 'hyphenated' society of democratic-welfare-capitalism) can be developed within the pluralist welfare state. A second weakness of Marshall's approach is that, in common with Fabians such as Titmuss, he too looks at social welfare largely from the standpoint of *consumption* and *distribution* and fails to explore its connection with *production*, at least in any direct sense. The result is a failure to grasp the problems specific to a capitalist market economy – profitability, accumulation, investment, international competitiveness and the like – which together with political pluralism and state welfare enable us to make sense of the current difficulties (including the problems of budget deficits and taxation). In his recent writings Marshall notes that the political economy of the post-war welfare state is in a 'precarious and somewhat battered condition', but shies away from any explanation.[26]

In short neither Titmuss's nor Marshall's intellectual legacy is of much help in coming to grips with the current problems of welfare capitalism as a social system and indicating possible lines of solution. Nor do we find social democrats outside Britain, at any rate in English-speaking countries, able to offer anything of substance on this score. The objectives of social welfare, whether they be maintaining a national minimum standard of living, achieving greater equality, or promoting altruism and community, need to be spelled out clearly and the prospect of their being achieved in the context of welfare capitalism also needs to be argued in detail. The relationship between economic and social welfare, and more generally between the requirements of a profit-oriented market economy and the values and institutions of social welfare, likewise need to be clarified. The relationship between the normative and the positive aspects of welfare, in particular the implications of the institutional dynamics resulting from the relative antonomy of the market economy, the plural polity and the welfare sector also need to be explored systematically. Put another way, the problem of the unintended consequences of one institutional sector for another must be addressed. These are among some of the major questions that need to be answered by a social democratic theory of the welfare state.

It is indeed something of a paradox that over three decades of successful welfare statism has not produced a 'Centrist' theory of the mixed system comparable to the analytical perspectives of the market liberals and Marxists. A part of the problem seems to be that the very pragmatism and reformism underlying the welfare state militates against a systematic theory of a mixed system comprised of market and state regulation. It is not easy to theorise about a system whose boundaries remain extremely fluid and whose paternity ranges from Bismarckian conservatism to modern social democracy, from New Deal liberalism to the 'political economy of the working class'. Moreover, if the welfare state is largely a product of piecemeal social (and moral?) engineering, then it may be futile to search for theoretical and normative coherence behind its patchwork quilt.

As Furniss and Tilton observe, 'To date no coherent and persuasive case for the welfare state exists. Its appeal is pretheoretical.... Instead of one satisfactory justification for the welfare state, a variety of partial and mutually inconsistent arguments circulate in the political debate of advanced industrial societies.'[27] Moreover, as they rightly point out, the absence of a clearcut logic to the welfare state is an intellectual rather than a political disadvantage. In modern democracies, to be persuasive a political argument must 'appeal to a variegated audience of citizens entertaining distinct and often contradictory fundamental assumptions.' What is required therefore 'is not strict logical consistency, but the capacity to elicit general agreement and support... current arguments for the welfare state have this broad, eclectic quality.'[28] What Furniss and Tilton forget to add is that these political advantages have the edge so long as the welfare state 'works'. When it runs into difficulties (as at present) then the lack of scientific and normative coherence becomes a distinct disadvantage (as at present) – at least as far as the *intellectual* defence of the middle ground is concerned.

Social Democratic Perspective

Whilst the current crisis has not evoked any major intellectual responses in defence of the post-war welfare state it has not been without its impact on social democratic thinking. In the following pages we shall look at some of the recent social democratic writings, relevant to our concerns, whether meant as a response to the current crisis or not. These may conveniently be grouped under four main headings: (i) Fabian socialism, (ii) moderate collectivism, (iii) neo-Keynesianism, and (iv) theoretical defence of the welfare state. Let us look at each of these briefly drawing mainly upon British works.

Fabian socialism
In the post-war years, social democratic strategy of change crystallised around a distributive and welfare-oriented socialism. Behind this strategy was the assumption of a post-capitalist Keynesian economy which would provide full employment and economic growth. Developments from about the mid-1970s have undermined this assumption. Chronic stagflation, rising unemployment and the failure of Keynesian techniques have dealt a body-blow to the strategy of financing social expenditure from economic growth and effecting some measure of redistribution of the growing national income in favour of the poor. More generally, the Fabian hope of using universal social services and progressive taxation as the means to a more equal society have been largely disappointed. Since about the late 1950s social scientists of varying shades and opinions have been unanimous in their view that taken together taxes and social services do little to reduce the inequality generated through the institutions of the market and private property.[29] Repeated attempts by Left Fabians in Britain to pressurise Labour governments into adopting redistributive tax policies appear to have yielded meagre results. Thus increasingly the poor have been asked to shoulder the burden of financing public expenditure.

The picture is no different when we turn from taxation to the social services. By providing education, health care and pensions on a universal basis it has been possible to avoid the stigma and low standards associated with a selective service; but it has also become quite clear that in a highly stratified society universally-available services often benefit the middle class more. Moreover, while free education and health care have been available for more than three decades, they seem to have had little effect in reducing class differentials in respect of educational and health outcomes. Overall, it would seem, the pursuit of equality and redistribution through universal services has not been particularly effective.

Thus, after a massive survey of poverty in Britain, Townsend concludes that redistribution is 'not much of a reality and the social services can increasingly be seen to... reinforce rather than reduce poverty and inequality.'[30] While social expenditure in Britain had risen appreciably as a percentage of the GNP, a great deal of poverty has persisted none the less. Le Grand's recent study, focused specifically on the redistributive impact of the services, reaches a similar conclusion: 'Public expenditure on the social services has not achieved equality in any of its interpretations. Public expenditure on health care, education, housing and transport systematically favours the better off, and thereby contributes to inequality in final outcome.'[31] Le Grand believes that behind the social democratic strategy of providing universal services was the desire to 'avoid the nettle of income redistribution'. It was an attempt to 'achieve such redistribution via the back door' which has clearly failed.[32] He concludes that in so far as equality is the aim, the problem must be tackled at its roots, i.e. the distribution of cash incomes must be made more equal.

Among the other weaknesses of the welfare state we might mention the adverse consequences of the growth of state bureaucracy and professional power. Over the years, the growing centralisation and bureaucratism involved in the provision of social security, health care and other services has come under increasing criticism. More recently, the success of the populist demagoguery of the Right against the encroachment of the state over people's lives has added a fresh point to this problem for many Fabians and friends of the welfare state. The relentless professionalisation of the services has also presented its own problems. Fabians have traditionally revered professionals – the 'Enlightened Ones' – and seen them as the progressive allies of the reformers. They have tended to associate professionalism with the idea of a service ethic and commitment to the disinterested use of knowledge for the benefit of the community.[33] Indeed, the enlightened paternalism underlying the Fabian approach, itself has a close affinity with professional orientation. Despite some criticism, therefore, on the whole a positive view of the professional role has been a part of social democratic thinking on social development.

Beginning from about the late 1960s radical sociology, which saw professionalism more as a strategy for the enhancement of income, status and power than as a reflection of a set of objective attributes of occupations, began to cast a critical eye on the professions.[34] Other arguments and evidence also began to accumulate to show that professionalism had a lot to do with vested interests. In the context of the social services, the professionals (especially the higher professions) are now seen as groups driving a hard bargain with government on salary and service conditions and trying to maximise their own sectional interests. Professionalism thus not only contributes to the rising cost of the service but by monopolising the provision and delivery of services, also makes the clients and lay people dependent on the professional.

Increasingly, Fabians are coming to recognise the force of these criticisms. Thus Townsend acknowledges the error and naivety of the belief prevalent in the 1960s that 'the more professionals we had the better ... the needs of democratic socialism would be served.' It has taken a long time – the 1960s and the 1970s – to 'begin to appreciate the kind of problems posed by managerialism and professionalism.'[35] Elsewhere, Townsend speaks of the role of the professions in reproducing inequality and privilege within the social services.

Frank Field, an ex-Labour MP and a well-known publicist on welfare issues, wrote in 1981 of the undesirable consequences of growing state power.[36] Under the strong influence of Crosland's pen social democracy had been equated with the pursuit of equality through state intervention. This process has given the state increasing power over the individual. Field does not deny that state regulation and provision of services may have promoted equality. But the same measures have also deprived individuals of the freedom to spend money as they like. They have been provided with more and more services – which they do not control, and on whose running they have no say. 'By ignoring the lessons of the technical limits on what the state can effectively do. Labour directly assists the Tories who have not been slow to capture public fears of state power and to fashion them into a campaign for a nightwatchman state.'[37]

Field, rather in the manner of a socialist Friedman, would like to see the state redistribute cash resources in favour of the lower income groups, rather than go on providing more and more services. Field believes that the state can be an effective instrument for transferring (redistributing) income and wealth. He goes on to propose a substantial reform of the taxation and social security systems which would eliminate poverty and redistribute income from the rich to the poor.[38] We shall return to this later. But let us note that in switching the emphasis from the services to the redistribution of income Field seems to be suggesting a fundamental re-orientation of social policy, for the provision of universal, as-of-right social services has formed a major plank in post-war social democratic policy. Unfortunately, Field does not discuss the services in his reform proposals and it is not clear if he favours their denationalisation so that, with more equal incomes, people might be free to choose and shop around as they do with other services at present.

But it is significant that Townsend, Le Grand and Field are all disenchanted with universal social services and favour a much more direct assault on inequality. Thus Townsend sees social policy in terms of three models: (i) 'Conditional welfare for the few', (ii) 'minimum rights for the many', and (iii) 'distributional justice for all'. These roughly form a continuum extending from the residual welfare of the conservatives to the 'national minimum' of Marshall and Beveridge, through to a socialist distributive approach which Townsend himself favours. Townsend finds that the principle of a national minimum, the model of social policy underlying the British welfare state, has proved difficult to put into practice. For 'there is an in-built tension, and even contradiction, in the application of the principle of a national minimum to a market economy. A minimum is hard to establish alongside or underneath a wage-earning and property-owning hierarchy – except at a very low level.'[39] In other words, the principle 'falls far short of the expectations of its advocates.'

Townsend's survey of Britain showed that poverty (relative deprivation) was widespread.[40] He recognises however that the conquest of poverty in this sense, and more generally the acceptance of the policy of 'distributive justice for all', would require a massive restructuring of society. It would involve, for example, the abolition of excessive wealth and income, abolition of unemployment (the institution of a legally enforceable right to work) and similar radical measures. By relating poverty to the wider structures of privilege and power, associated *inter alia* with occupation and property, Townsend shows that abolition of poverty would require a far deeper social change than has generally been believed.[41] In this sense Townsend's work goes far beyond the bounds of social democratic thinking, based on modest redistribution of incomes and the provision of generous social services financed out of growth.

In differing ways Field, Le Grand and Townsend all seem to be moving away from what might be called Crosland's welfare socialism. At the same time, however, some of the basic elements of the Fabian approach persist. First, there is no link between the social and economic in the social structure, or more precisely between distribution and the productive organisation of society. Thus Field proposes a thorough reform of virtually the entire system of income distribution and taxation in order to bring about greater equality. Yet he makes no attempt to consider the implications of such a distributive strategy for the system of production which, presumably, is to remain in private hands and function through the market mechanism. Townsend, too, while grounding his analysis of poverty in the class structure and the market economy fails to consider the relationship between radical changes in distribution of the kind he proposes, and the system of production based on profitability, material incentives and the freedom of an international market economy.

Consider, for example, the implications of the legal right to employment, which Townsend advocates, for the capitalist market economy. Such a measure would have massive implications for the productive system. In short, is it possible to socialise distribution while production remains in private hands? The implications of the current crisis of capitalism, which has brought back mass unemployment and shown itself incapable of even providing 'minimum rights for the many', seem to be that no radical programme of social distribution can be taken seriously if it fails to address the problem of production and the control of economic resources. Indeed many democratic socialists have become increasingly aware of the need to attack the problem of inequality at its roots, i.e. in the very system of production, specifically at the level of wages and the organisation of work. The current crisis of welfare capitalism has underlined the need to address the problems of the economy, above all those of production and growth, if distributive issues are to be solved and social justice secured. Thus it is not enough to say that 'far from putting economic objectives like solutions for inflation or economic growth at the head of the list of national concerns, we should put social objectives like social equality or the abolition of poverty at the forefront of our national effort.'[42]

Another weakness of Fabian thinking has been the tendency to ignore 'subjective' facts about the social structure. Since Fabianism has meant essentially *administrative* (rather than political) solutions to social problems, only facts relevant to such an approach have been looked for and emphasised. Social facts have referred almost exclusively to occupation, income and demographic characteristics rather than to the attitudes and beliefs of the subjects themselves, the poor, the deprived, the workers. It is to the credit of Townsend and his researchers that they did probe into people's own attitudes toward poverty. What they found however offers cold comfort to Fabian reformers. As Townsend admits, there is 'much more inclination among the working class to have individualistic explanations of poverty and to imagine that people are poor because of personal mismanagement rather than the institutional structures of society.'[43] Indeed, it appears that the British take a much more personalised view of the causes of poverty compared with the Swedes and other Europeans.[44] As Townsend concedes, 'It's clear that political education has been far less influential in the history of the labour movement than many of us supposed.'[45]

Many Labourites now recognise the importance of popular attitudes and beliefs, and of consciousness and ideology, for social reform. Le Grand writes:

The lesson is clear. If greater equality of whatever kind is desired it is necessary to reduce economic inequality. To do this successfully, however, it is necessary to reduce the hold of the ideology of inequality on people's value and beliefs . . . . Ideology is a much more important determinant of social processes than is often supposed.[46]

Clearly the agenda for changing people's beliefs and values about inequality, in a society steeped in hereditary privilege and social deference beginning with the monarchy and the court, is a much wider one than that of administrative reform. Field, in more traditional Fabian vein, asserts that there is a 'moral case for a significant vertical redistribution of income from the rich to poor'.[47] This may be evident to Field and his fellow Fabians, but is it to the majority of British people? After all, Field's own book starts with observation that 'laziness' and 'drink' were among the most frequently cited causes of poverty by the British in a recent survey of EEC countries.

The election to power of Thatcher, with the support of skilled manual workers concerned about eroding wage differentials, the large support for the middle-of-the-road Social Democratic Party in Britain, and the jingoism connected with the Falklands invasion in 1982 are hardly portents of growing egalitarianism. Meacher, for example, recognises the importance of the problem. On the prospects of democratic socialism in the 1980s he writes:

At present little is being done to educate and mobilise socialists in Britain, as is illustrated most strikingly perhaps by the virtual absence of a socialist press. Until much more is done, it is certain that the grip of the dominant value system will be strengthened further still, and the ideological supremacy of the Establishment will be even more firmly consolidated.[48]

Meanwhile Fabian collectivism can do little more than maintain its moral stance and reiterate what social policy in Britain *ought* to be doing ('we *must*', etc.), and propose administrative solutions, even while the gap between these noble sentiments and expectations and the harsh reality under Thatcherite capitalism grows wider every day. Fabianism, largely a form of administrative and distributive socialism, seems to be at its best when times are good economically. For then its chief method, namely social engineering through *consensus*, in turn based on fact-finding and a diffuse appeal to the values of community, justice, compassion and the like, seems to work. These favourable times also nurture the belief that more might be achieved through such means. The crisis of capitalist economy alters the situation radically, making it clear that what are at bottom structural problems (rooted in the economic system and class power) cannot be solved administratively. Every major capitalist crisis – that of the 1930s, for example – therefore cuts the very ground from under the feet of Fabian collectivism. The current crisis is no exception.

Moderate collectivism
A rather different response to the problems of welfare capitalism has been to advocate a moderate form of collectivism, one that will have a clear rationale within the context of a market economy and would therefore 'fit' the system better. In Britain the names of Marshall, Robson and Pinker are associated with such a viewpoint. While these writers differ in many ways in their approach, the thread of moderate collectivism running through their recent work provides an obvious link.

Marshall, as we noted earlier, finds that the composite social formation of democratic-welfare-capitalism has not been working well for some time. The welfare idea has been degraded as well as downgraded, largely because the respective spheres of the market economy and social welfare have been increasingly blurred. Marshall believes a thriving market economy to be a vital component of an efficient, democratic society. At the same time social welfare, especially in the form of universal services (e.g. health care and education) remains a necessity, providing a framework of prevention against poverty and helping to create a civilised community.[49] Here Marshall's idea that the state welfare services are a part of the status of citizenship in modern society provides the underlying rationale for a national minimum. However, the gentle prose in which he speaks of 'Strengthening . . . the civilising power of welfare'[50] tends to gloss over such features of these services as increasing professional dominance and rising costs. Health care is the prime example here, although to a lesser extent education and the personal social services are relevant too. If a citizenship approach requires that these services be provided to everyone at an optimum standard, then it is only the income maintenance programme, consisting of cash transfers, that emerges as one that might be scaled down in terms of scope and expenditure. But the exact policy implications of moderate collectivism in the area of income maintenance remain unclear.

Unlike the Left Fabians Marshall openly acknowledges, indeed emphasises, the economic component in welfare. Not only the social services but the economy too contributes to welfare in the wider sense. Social welfare, therefore, must not be allowed to interfere with or hinder the economy. And if the division of labour between the two spheres is generally accepted (consensus over the role of social policy?), then the composite social system of democracy-welfare-capitalism might not only survive but also be strengthened.[51] Clearly, Marshall has a great deal of sympathy with the national minimum view of welfare, embodied for example in the Beveridge Report, which fits in with the notion of citizenship and the ethos of an egalitarian civic culture. This has little to do with the pursuit of equality and redistribution which, for Marshall, belongs to a very different area of social action. To confound these various objectives is to dilute and degrade the essence of welfare.

Marshall uses the same distinction in his attempt to rescue poverty from the embrace of inequality. In the ideal democratic-welfare-capitalist society, 'poverty is a disease' but inequality is 'an essential structural feature'. Poverty can therefore be abolished in such a society. Marshall admits that poverty forms a part of the wider social question of inequality, but rejects the notion 'that one could not eradicate poverty without solving "the problem of inequality".'[53] Selectivity and means tests again are instruments that Marshall would not reject out of hand: they are not necessarily stigmatising. Marshall has held some of these views publicly for a long time. Others he has come to espouse more explicitly only in recent years.

Robson, too, is concerned with the degradation of the welfare idea, with the loss of direction of the welfare state. As noted above, he is greatly disturbed by the lack of a normative (and by implication also scientific) theory of social welfare. Not unlike Marshall, he believes that some form of national consensus on the objectives of social welfare is essential if the welfare state is to constitute a stable and viable social system.[54] Moreover, Robson stresses the importance of popular attitudes and feelings concerning social issues in their bearing on welfare. This is a welcome emphasis all too rare in the administratively-oriented literature in this area. Commenting on the dearth of ideas about the objectives of the welfare state Robson notes that the advocacy of equality has become the conventional wisdom of the Left. But how widespread is the belief in equality in British society? Fabian advocates of equality rarely ask that question. Moroever, observes Robson, relative definitions of poverty have merged almost imperceptibly with those of inequality. Whereas the idea of a national minimum has been the 'cornerstone of welfare state policy', the pursuit of equality introduces a radically different aim within the fabric of the welfare state.[55] He too believes that 'genuine' poverty can be (has been?) abolished within the welfare state. Like Marshall he maintains that the mixed economy and the various economic liberties that go with it have to be seen as desirable features of these societies. Unfortunately, Robson's own normative view of welfare, couched in extremely general terms, does not take us far. What, for example, are we to make of the statement that the welfare state is (i.e. ought to be) concerned with the 'well-being of the whole society'? or that it is (i.e. ought to be) 'Committed to a continuous improvement of the social services in regard to their scope, adequacy and quality.'[56] In short Robson, like Marshall, finds it difficult to be precise about the role of the welfare state.

Pinker, a leading British social administrator, has also broken with Titmuss-type collectivism and the idea of the pursuit of equality through social policy. He favours moderate forms of social protection which instead of being at daggers drawn with the market economy will live in harmony with it and be more in keeping with the sentiments and feelings of the British people. For Pinker too an efficient and healthy market economy, personal liberties and democracy are essential parts of the broader fabric of welfare. He evokes the Keynes-Beveridge tradition of thinking about welfare quite explicitly in support of his position.[57]

What moderate collectivists leave out of account, however,

is the social dynamics of the welfare system. It is one thing to advance moderate collectivism as a normative proposition, although as we have seen there are problems even at this level. It is quite another to demonstrate that a delineated sphere of social welfare could, as it were, be sustained within the context of a market economy and plural polity without either degenerating into a residual form of welfare or simply continuing to grow (as the post-war welfare state did from its modest Beveridgian beginnings) under the pressure of demography, relative price effect, political market, professional-bureaucratic interests, and the like. Put simply, these views are plausible at the normative level but not at the level of practice.

A part of the problem is that none of these social scientists really examines the dynamics of a social system which comprises a market economy, a pressure group polity and a state welfare sector. Since market capitalism and interest-group politics are pre-eminently about the pursuit of self-interest (in the economic and political market-place, respectively) the social welfare sector (the junior partner in this trio of economics-politics-welfare) simply becomes a part of the value system and structure of the wider society. Is this not the problem identified, for example, by both Hirsch and Bell (see pp. 126-7 above)? In sum, the moderates fail to address the *institutional* problem of how to build and maintain consensus in a pluralist welfare state.

Moderate collectivism has other weaknesses. First, it fails to see the role of the state and the social welfare system in relation to changing technological and economic factors. Thus, in the 1980s, the possibility of large-scale unemployment and the inability of the market economy to provide jobs for millions has to be considered when arguing for moderate collectivism.

Second, the implications of moderate collectivism or a 'national minimum' concept for the various services (e.g. income maintenance, health, education, housing) need to be spelled out.

Third, the reasons for advocating a limited role for social welfare must be made quite clear. There is sometimes an assumption, more or less implicit, behind these arguments that rising social expenditure and the attitudes generated by the

143

security of full employment and social welfare more generally are responsible for Britain's ills, especially her economic decline. The dubious nature of this assumption is obvious. A cursory glance at big spenders like West Germany or Sweden makes it amply clear that public expenditure on health, education and welfare does not *ipso facto* lead to a decline in productivity or economic growth. Indeed judged by the proportion of GNP spent on the social services in advanced industrial countries Britain's collectivism is now definitely modest.[58] Thus there is a need to clarify the nature and rationale of moderate collectivism.

Fourth, and a related point, is that the issue of national consensus over welfare (social and economic) is quite different from that of the degree of collectivism. As countries like Austria and Sweden amply demonstrate consensus, stability and growth can be achieved within welfare capitalism at a fairly high level of collectivism. The issues of consensus and the degree of collectivism must not be conflated.

Neo-Keynesianism

While some social democrats have been repeating their moral prescription about what must be done to further social justice and equality others have been reaffirming a belief in neo-Keynesianism. A recent collection of Fabian writings[59] provides a good example of this approach which involves essentially a reflationary strategy ('reflation in one country') based on increased public expenditure. This is expected to create jobs and generate demand for the output of private industry. But it is also admitted that 'improvements in living standards, including the standards of public services can only come about through increased efficiency and productivity.'[60] The anti-inflationary thrust of this warning is quite clear. Moreover, it virtually affirms the Croslandian approach to social expenditure, based on growth and higher output, in contrast with the Left Fabian approach which looks for a redistribution of incomes (from the rich to the poor) through the social welfare system. It is also acknowledged that we cannot 'expand public spending by as much as we like for ever.'[61] Thus some sort of a limit on government spending, however unspecified, is recognised as well as the mixed nature of the economy. More important, it is assumed that 'the promise of a commitment to bring back full employment will make the advantages of greater productivity clear to everyone. It should remove the fear that one man's productivity gain is another man's job loss.'[62] This is wishful thinking when we know that precisely the opposite seems to have been true of Britain's thirty years' experience of full employment. In the main, neo-Keynesian thinking of this kind relies on the strategy of generating economic growth, part of which could then be allocated to social programmes and priorities. Hence a scheme of investment and industrial development through the National Enterprise Board is also seen as important.

It is difficult to take such facile solutions to the problems of British welfare capitalism (unemployment, inflationary wage settlement, over-manning, productivity, growth) seriously. There is a distinctly *déjà vu* air about these pronouncements. Despite some new features (e.g. import tariffs) relevant to the 1980s it is, in essence, a plan (not unlike the Mitterand programme in France) that the British Labour Party has tried before. Its approach to social expenditure is also a familiar one, although it recognises fully the scarcity of resources as well as the need to restrain, or even reduce, social spending in some areas.

This neo-Keynesian – and one might add also Croslandian – approach, for example, informs Labour Party's outline of economic and social policy, *Labour's Programme 1982*. It is based on a strategy through which it is hoped that growth will be resumed, full employment restored and social policy objectives met. Yet this approach, and the attendant optimism, flies in the face of the general trend of rising unemployment and economic stagnation in most European economies. In the absence of growth, increased productivity (one of the objectives of the programme) is likely to result in higher unemployment. Indeed it looks as if large-scale unemployment will continue to be a feature of British and other western economies. As Jordan points out, 'Labour, while seeming to have turned away from the optimism of Anthony Crosland's vision, has in fact clung on to many of its most unrealistic features. Above all, *Programme 1982* continuously asserts that there are no hard choices to be made; that redistribution will

145

occur painlessly, through growth, and with the restoration of full employment.'[63] Clearly British Fabianism, like a great deal else in Britain, seems to be mired in traditionalism and can offer little that is new. It is not surprising that Mrs Thatcher not only champions the cause of the people against the Big State but also takes pride in her 'realism' compared with the facile optimism of many of her political opponents.

Against orthodoxy, from the somewhat jaded Old World Fabianism, we turn to a refreshingly original as well as hardheaded analysis of the current impasse by Lester Thurow.[64] Thurow's work merits attention for a variety of reasons, not least for being one of the most impressive arguments put forward by an *American* political economist from a Centre-Left position. Thurow focuses on the US economy, but his reasoning applies more generally to advanced capitalist economies. His main point is that the US has reached a point where further economic growth requires major adjustments, in respect of energy use, industrial investment, and the like. In this process of structural change some groups stand to lose while others stand to gain. It is a zero-sum game in which there are no winners without corresponding losers.

But thanks to the political economy of the welfare state – post-war developments in democracy, government responsibility for protecting living standards, and the growth of interest groups including those representing the under-privileged – it has become increasingly difficult if not virtually impossible to impose the costs of change on any particular group in society, at least not of the magnitude necessary for economic growth to be feasible. That is the essence of the current impasse. In Thurow's words,

> For most of our problems there are several solutions. But all these solutions have the characteristic that someone must suffer large economic losses. No one wants to volunteer for this role, and we have a political process that is incapable of forcing anyone to shoulder this burden. Everyone wants someone else to suffer the necessary economic losses, and as a consequence none of the possible solutions can be adopted.[65]

Thurow examines a range of issues including energy, inflation, government regulation of the economy, growth and income distribution. He is able to argue quite convincingly that big government and budget deficits are not at the root of inflation and economic stagnation. Hence the nostrums of the Right, including lower taxes for the wealthy, reduced public spending, and so on, as well as being inequitable, are irrelevant to the main problem. He points out, for example, that many European countries have a far bigger and more pervasive government than the US but none the less, have achieved a high level of economic growth. 'Government absorbs slightly over 30 per cent of the GNP in the United States, but over 50 per cent of the GNP in West Germany. Fifteen other countries collect a large fraction of the GNP in taxes.'[66] Nor have the United States' competitors 'unleashed work effort and savings' through increased income differentials. Using the earnings ratio between the top and the bottom decile as an index, 'the West Germans work hard with 36 per cent less inequality... the Japanese work even harder with 50 per cent less inequality.'[67] Indeed, among industrial nations only the French surpass Americans in inequality of earnings.

Furthermore, the history of such countries as West Germany and Sweden, as well as the United States' own experience (since the New Deal), shows that far from hindering growth, government intervention and social welfare programmes seem to have aided it. As regards inflation, Thurow believes that the major influence in the 1970s was the sharp rise in oil prices (OPEC decisions) albeit the Vietnam war and the US government's energy policy were also to blame. Inflation in later years, it is true, reflects the inability (or unwillingness) of governments to impose the costs of oil price rises on any one segment of society (although inflation has its own redistributive impact). But the idea that inflation is caused largely through government growth, budget deficits and high wages is both simplistic and misleading. The situation is rather more complex:

Energy, growth, and inflation are interrelated on many fronts. Without growing energy supplies, economic growth is difficult, and rapidly rising energy prices provide a powerful inflationary force. Inflation leads to public policies that produce idle capacity and severely retard growth.[68]

147

But economic growth in the 1980s requires, above all, major structural changes. New industries have to rise and old ones decline. Thus investment as well as 'disinvestment' (i.e. running down old unprofitable industries), becomes essential. Yet interest-group politics and government intervention makes disinvestment difficult: 'Instead of adopting public policies to speed up the process of disinvestment, we act to slow it down with protection and subsidies for the inefficient.'[69] Many industries in the USA enjoy protection in one form or another. Shipbuilding for example is 'completely dependent upon subsidies'. All such actions are meant to provide economic security, but lock the economy in low productivity areas. Without effective disinvestment it is virtually impossible to compete in the modern growth race. Moreover, workers fear that technical change will take their jobs away and alternative work will be hard to find. They therefore push for more restrictive work rules to stop technical progress. 'The end result is a stagnating economy with a productivity slowdown.'[70]

For Thurow, it is this issue of interdependence between capital and labour that goes unrecognised in facile, free-market solutions. If the labour force is indifferent or uncooperative then investment in new plant and equipment may not prove very productive (and therefore not profitable).

New skills and higher earnings depend upon a co-operative work force. Simply raising the income of capitalists, with tax cuts that must be paid for with tax increases for workers, is unlikely to achieve either more investment or a higher growth of productivity.... Starting a class war is hardly the way to proceed.[71]

Thurow uses the Japanese lifetime employment system, where technological change and higher productivity do not threaten either jobs or earnings, based largely on a mixture of seniority and profit-related bonus, as an example of a positive relationship between job security on the one hand and technological change and productivity on the other. In pointing this out, however, Thurow's main objective is to illustrate 'the complexity of the problem and the irrelevance of simple one-factor solutions'.[72]

Thurow offers no panacea for the ills besetting US capitalism, let alone for welfare capitalism more generally. If anything his insistence on the 'societal' or 'systemic' nature of the issues warns us against quick fixes and miracle cures, such as those touted by monetarists. Rather it is his stress on the inter-related and interdependent nature of the problems (and their solutions) that commands respect. For example, he does not treat either production or distribution in isolation from each other.

As a social democrat Thurow believes that the costs of social change cannot be allowed to lie where they fall. In order to free the economy from the impasse in which it finds itself, the impact of change must be cushioned. The government has an important role to play in spreading the burden of change equitably and sheltering individuals from the negative impact of change.

Thurow believes that since the US prides itself on the work ethic the government must take responsibility for providing everyone who wants a job with one, if necessary through a federal guaranteed job programme. Moreover, the government should act to reduce, or at least prevent from worsening, the level of inequality of incomes, mainly through progressive taxation. Unlike many Fabian and Leftist writers on welfare who purport to show that the social services do not help the poor and then proceed to ask for more state welfare, Thurow maintains that without transfer payments and forms of welfare assistance, including food stamps, the standard of living of the elderly, the poor and other low income groups would have been much worse. He gives other examples of the progressive nature of the public sector. For example, because of its equit-able practices blacks and women stand a much better chance of being hired and their pay differentials, compared with white males, also tend to be smaller.

Thurow does not, however, favour government regulation of everything. Eschewing dogma, he argues that the choice is not between regulation or its total absence but between the right and the wrong kinds of regulation. Echoing the argu-ments of Bell and Hirsch (see pp. 126-7), Thurow believes that decisions concerning equity and distribution can no longer be fudged. Unlike these writers, however, he does take a stand. He offers his own version, admittedly somewhat pragmatic, of equity principles. For example, he suggests as the effective poverty line half the average income as the level below which no one should be expected to live. He argues for a more progressive tax structure. He suggests a differential of 5:1 between top and bottom quintile of earnings, existing at present among *white males* in full-time work, as the maximum for *all* workers. This compares with a current differential of 27:1 for the American labour force as a whole, that is including women and blacks. To cushion the impact of economic and technical change Thurow advocates giving help to individuals (retraining, relocation, financial assistance) rather than subsidising industries or firms.[74] These principles are important, for unlike orthodox neo-Keynesians Thurow does not believe in a miraculous return of growth which will automatically benefit everyone. Nor does he look for corporatist solutions as such. He rejects mandatory wages and prices control arguing, quite rightly, that these measures can only work if voluntary. Moreover, he notes, only about a quarter of the labour force is unionised in the USA, a level of unionisation rather low to be conducive to a corporatist approach.

Yet there is little doubt that, overall, Thurow's approach represents a move away from the pluralist welfare state (DWS, see pp. 102-3) towards one that has elements of corporatism (IWS, see pp. 102-3). Unlike the pluralist (DWS) approach which differentiates social policy clearly and sees it as something apart from economic policy (e.g. Titmuss, Beveridge, Marshall, etc.), Thurow sees them as closely interrelated. Secondly, in line with the corporatist approach (IWS), he sees institutional or systemic integration as interdependent with group integration. In other words, if economic problems are to be solved successfully then inter-group relations, centred on distribution and equity claims, must be resolved.

In this sense his approach to social management is systematic (as in the IWS) rather than piecemeal (as in the DWS). Thurow does not discuss the social services (e.g. health care and education), as such. But in the area of economic investment, job creation, transfer payments, progressive taxation and the like he envisions more rather than less government responsibility. Unlike neo-conservatives, Thurow does not believe a return to *laisser-faire* either possible or desirable. Neither does he believe moderate collectivism to be the answer. His analysis shows quite clearly that social welfare can no longer be meaningfully isolated from economic welfare. Moreover, if equity considerations are not to be set aside then government must involve itself more (or rather differently) not less with economic regulation and welfare in its wider sense. In these key respects his thinking goes beyond post-war Keynesianism. Unlike many neo-Keynesians and orthodox Fabians he recognises that the option of generating full employment and economic growth through a managed market economy and then using social welfare (the role of social policy in post-war years) to redistribute and socialise growth is no longer available. The problems of democratic-welfare-capitalism cannot now be solved in the manner of Croslandian social democracy, or for that matter a Beveridgian national minimum.

Thurow's main weakness lies in his ability to specify the institutional mechanism through which consensus, or at least major support, could be built around the kind of approach he advocates. He bemoans the absence of a European-style political system in the USA in which the ideological divide between parties is clear cut and governments are elected with a mandate to carry out a clearly identifiable set of policies.[75] He has a point here in that the absence of a Social Democratic Party in the US frustrates certain kinds of development. But the experience of Western Europe makes it quite clear that without a broad consensus among the major economic power-holders economic growth, equity and welfare, and political democracy cannot be combined successfully.

However, these critical remarks should not detract from the boldness, originality and sociological realism of his analysis. The label neo-Keynesian may be quite inappropriate for his economic and social approach. But the attempt to go beyond prevailing orthodoxies in the analysis of contemporary problems, an openly espoused value position, the attempt to link means and ends clearly, the belief in a mixed economy and liberal democracy, and lastly the insistence on value choices are all reminiscent of Keynes's response to the crisis of capitalism in the 1930s. In any case, what matters is the content rather than the label. And there is little doubt that the political economy of the welfare state presented by Thurow is one of the most original (without being idiosyncratic) and persuasive to appear in the Centre-Left tradition in recent years.

Theoretical defence of the welfare state

In recent years the intellectual foundations of social democracy and the welfare state have come under heavy critical fire. Generally speaking, criticisms of the welfare abound, whereas its systematic defence is hard to come by. From this viewpoint the recent contributions of Room, and Furniss and Tilton merit particular attention.[76] From somewhat differing perspectives and concerns they advance a range of arguments in defence of the Centre-Left view of social policy. We shall consider these arguments in some detail and comment on their validity as well as adequacy, beginning with Room's work.

Room examines the view of social policy in modern western society held by three major theoretical perspectives – liberalism, Marxism and social democracy. He looks at the interpretation of social policy and social change offered by each from an historical perspective. The development of social policy in modern British society forms the testing ground, the laboratory so to speak, for the interpretation offered by these theories. Overall, Room finds the social democratic perspective to be the most convincing of the three.[77] In so far as he is sympathetic to the social democratic paradigm of social policy and also considers its merits and demerits in some detail his work is most timely. A critical defence of the social democratic position could be of considerable interest especially in the light of the current difficulties of the welfare state.

However Room looks at the various theories in the context of the historical development of capitalism. He is not concerned with the current crisis of social democracy and the welfare state. The absence of a focus on current problems robs the book of a good deal of contemporary relevance and the arguments advanced remain largely academic. In some important areas of contemporary debate the book is either out of date or else its assumptions have been invalidated. In respect of others Room practically admits that social democracy can offer little by way of a solution to current difficulties.[78] Let us look at an example of the former. Following the analysis of economists like Kaldor in the 1960s, Room maintains that economic growth no longer depends on the rate of investment and profitability (accumulation of capital). Rather in economies like the British, which have reached a position of labour scarcity (!)[79] it is the skill and expertise of the labour force that becomes crucial for economic growth. Therefore Room concludes that it is the social policy of the state, which helps create a healthy and skilled labour force, that is now crucial for growth rather than investment and profitability. Room admits that rising unemployment seems to question Kaldor's view of increasing labour scarcity in advanced capitalist societies. But he suggests that 'if we regard the current international recession as short run and as signifying no necessary fundamental change in the pattern of western economic development' (a massive assumption which, to put it mildly, looks increasingly unrealistic) then Kaldor's 'emphasis on labour scarcity in manufacturing industry as a developing constraint in economic growth will remain valid.'[80]

The point is this: even if the recession had turned out to be a temporary one (in the manner of previous post-war recessions), thus validating Room's assumptions, there would still remain serious problems with his argument. Writing in the 1970s, it is somewhat unreal to put forward labour scarcity as the major reason for Britain's poor economic performance compared to other industrialised economies. Rather, one would have to speak of labour market rigidities, over-manning, trade union attitudes towards new technology and lack of investment in advanced technology in British industry. Here one could argue that the policies of full employment and social security combined with traditional defensive trade union attitudes may have a lot to do with the poor state of the British economy. In short, far from helping the cause of growth social policy may in fact have been hindering it.

But quite apart from the problems of British economy, what happens to social democratic argument about state's role in promoting growth when the recession turns into a long drawn stagnation, if not an outright depression (after Room has dismissed Marx's gloomy prognostications as outmoded)? In the 1930s the Webbs, those quintessential Fabians, eventually turned to Soviet-style communism as the only solution to capitalism's ills. Time and time again the capitalistic nature of western economies has proved to be the bane of social democratic hopes of an evolutionary socialism. The 1980s seem to be no exception.

Room's own view of the prospects for a social democratic advance, in the light of current difficulties of capitalism, is quite pessimistic. 'In the present situation of recession and public expenditure cuts.... The Social Democrats' hope of translating privileges into universal social rights are rendered increasingly difficult.'[81] Furthermore, 'what has for several decades been taken as perhaps the most well-established universal social right – that to employment – has increasingly been translated into a privilege of the more powerful.'[82] Finally, to cap it all, these and other developments 'seem to signify the erosion of altruism and moral solidarity in the face of the shared [?] adversity – an erosion that political leaders and those groups wielding power in the wider society (including the trade unions) have promoted, whether by intent or neglect.'[83] Here we seem to be back to square one with Marx's reserve army of labour coming to life, altruism disappearing, and a *sauve qui peut* mentality taking over with social welfare facing a bleak prospect.

Room draws attention to many shortcomings and problems connected with the practice of the welfare state either ignored or not foreseen by social democrats, e.g. vested professional and bureaucratic interests, opportunism of political leaders, the ability of vested interests more generally to thwart reforms, the 'unprincipled nature of the wider distribution of power and advantage' and its implications for altruistic social policies.[84] But he is unable to offer any solutions apart from pointing out that if the prospects for a 'social democratic commonwealth', look bleak such a development is not inevitable. Such 'a future will not have come inevitably, but to some degree will rather have been the fruit of decisions by political leaders and, indeed, by the citizenry at large that centre in their lack of commitment to a promotive [?] social policy.'[85] Thus, in the long haul, the social democratic view of society and social policy may have the edge over liberalism and Marxism. But in the short haul social democrats (actual and potential) are left more or less to fend for themselves (theoretically speaking) in the midst of rising unemployment, growing sectionalism and shrinking altruism.

Although Room's approach to his subject-matter is comprehensive and the treatment systematic, his analysis none the less suffers from a number of defects. First, it focuses almost entirely on problems of social integration (and that too from the viewpoint of citizenship and the democratic polity while neglecting the cash nexus entailed in industrial and property relationships under capitalism), and fails to consider problems of system integration adequately. In other words, the focus is almost entirely on values, social relationships and the moral basis of community, while problems of the technical-economic functioning of society are largely ignored. The book scarcely mentions the Depression, the trade-cycle and other awkward capitalist entities which brought the economy to near collapse in the 1930s, contributed mightily to the growth of Fascism, and eventually led to the outbreak of war. Faced with the crisis of capitalist economy in the 1930s, British social democracy could offer little.

More serious still is Room's omission of any reference to Keynesianism. (The index contains no reference to Keynes, and as far as I can see the importance of Keynesian techniques in maintaining full employment – one of the 'social rights' of citizenship – is completely overlooked.) Admittedly, a sociological work such as Room's cannot be expected to discuss economic issues in any detail. It remains true none the less that Room falls victim to the cardinal sin of Fabian writings on welfare – namely, the failure to consider adequately the productive aspects of capitalist economy and their relationship to social reform and the welfare state. The failure to acknowledge the centrality of the market economy for capitalist society and the failure to consider problems of system integration mean that the importance of the relationship between system and social integration, for the success of the 'middle path' of mixed economy and the welfare state (see Chapter 4), is missed completely. Despite attempts at a social structural analysis Room's approach to his subject-matter remains essentially idealist. He focuses on values and the ability of the social democratic movement to persuade the citizenry and the organised interests to choose the right values. Support for the appropriate values and policies then emerges as the 'solution' to the difficulties facing the welfare state – not exactly a helpful analysis for social democrats, or others for that matter.

A cogent defence of the modern welfare state, typified by Sweden, is offered by Furniss and Tilton. It is based on the rejection of both the 'liberal strategy of free and unregulated markets' as well as the 'traditional socialist nostrum of nationalization'.[86] The free-market economy fails to achieve equilibrium, provide full employment and ensure social justice and efficiency. Nationalisation, on the other hand, as the experience of Britain and other countries shows quite clearly, does not help realise the traditional socialist aspirations. Moreover as Soviet bloc countries amply demonstrate 'state socialism can be more tyrannous than private capitalism.'[87] By focusing on Sweden as the model welfare state Furniss and Tilton are able to present a strong case for the irrelevance of nationalisation, since in Sweden the extent of public ownership of industry is extremely limited. Social democracy has chosen the path of regulating private economy and providing social welfare rather than extending public ownership.

Furniss and Tilton use a threefold typology to analyse modern forms of state intervention in economic and social affairs: the 'positive state', the 'social security state', and the 'social welfare state'. Only the latter two really qualify as welfare states. Of the three types, the USA provides an example of the first, Britain the second, and Sweden the third. The 'positive state' aims 'primarily at insuring economic stability and thus the self-interest of existing property holders'. The 'social security state' aims at 'a guaranteed national minimum'. The 'social welfare state', with which Furniss and Tilton's sympathies really lie, aims at furthering 'greater social and economic equality' and collective participation in the making of public policy. These are ideal-type formulations and the USA, Britain and Sweden are seen as empirical cases more or less approximating these three forms of state intervention.

Furniss and Tilton spell out the values underlying the social welfare state and also seek to demonstrate the technical viability and success of countries like Sweden in moving towards the model of the social welfare state. They also consider, rather briefly, some of the major arguments levelled against the welfare state by its critics, both conservative and radical, but tend to dismiss them rather lightly.[88] Be that as it may, Furniss and Tilton's work deserves to be recognised more widely in social policy literature, as it is one of the few examples of a systematic defence of the welfare state. Moreover it is admirable in its clarity, economy, balance between the empirical and ideational, and openly-stated value premises underlying its arguments. It also offers an interesting typology of state intervention. As I suggest below, the notion of the 'social welfare state' has distinct affinity with the idea of the corporatist welfare state (see Chapter 4). Yet despite its many strengths, Furniss and Tilton's work remains weak on contemporary relevance. Essentially it pre-dates the present crisis and therefore does not confront some of the key issues that have arisen within the last five years or so which have forced the welfare state very much on the defensive. For example, Furniss and Tilton defend state intervention in the market economy on the Keynesian grounds that the capitalist market economy is not self-regulating and therefore needs 'a visible public hand to steer it'.[89] They counter the conservative critique by referring to the success of the mixed economy and the welfare state. The 'end result of the superiority of public and private co-operation over a reliance on private rationality alone has been demonstrated concretely in the upsurge of prosperity since World War II, by the disinclination of any major political party in any western nation to revert to pre-Depression economic practices, and by the advent of the "post-market" economy. To use Shonfield's phrase, "wisely managed capitalism" has become the order of the day with the emphasis as much on "managed" as on "capitalism".'[90] Here we are still in the golden age of postwar affluence and the welfare state, with stagflation no more than a small cloud over the horizon. Indeed Furniss and Tilton's reference to inflation is primarily academic and concerns the modest inflationary pressures typical of the 1960s.

Their rebuttal of the Left ('Radical') critique suffers from a similar defect. It does not take into account the economic recession and the crisis of production facing the capitalist economy which has given fresh point to the Marxist critique of social democracy and welfarism. Thus they belittle the problem of profitability in a capitalist economy. They also misunderstand the nature of the Marxist argument in suggesting that it is based on 'a faulty psychological assumption', that 'the capitalist's fundamental desire...is to make profits.'[91] The systemic problems of the capitalist market economy, as evident in the decline of profitability, does not feature in their discussion. The issue of 'fiscal crisis', (i.e. mounting budget deficits, rising public expenditure, high rates of taxation) is similarly played down. More generally, they endorse the classic social democratic tenet, namely, that distribution can be socialised while leaving production in the hands of private capitalism albeit of a managed kind.[92]

Finally, we should mention that Furniss and Tilton seem to assume too readily that the state apparatus functions is a *rational* instrument of policy. They dismiss the notion of vested professional and bureaucratic interests somewhat lightly. They also fail to consider the general problem that in a pressure group polity the state, rather than being a guardian of the public interest, becomes a vehicle through which sectional interests realise their aims. Virtually nothing is said about the feminist charge of patriarchy against the welfare state. (No doubt Furniss and Tilton could argue that the problem of sexism in social policy can be taken care of within the parameters of the welfare state. Here Sweden could once again provide a positive model.)

In sum, given the 'pre-crisis' nature of Furniss and Tilton's study it fails to address the emergent problems of welfare capitalism in some crucial areas – the failure of Keynesian techniques, and the advent of stagflation and unemployment. The key assumptions underlying the book – the success of mixed economy and the efficacy of Keynesian management techniques – give it a somewhat *passé* flavour.

Both Room, and Furniss and Tilton produce cogent arguments in support of the social democratic view of social change by way of the welfare state. But these arguments rely on either an historical view of the evolution of capitalism (Room), or on the success of Keynesian welfare capitalism (Furniss and Tilton). Neither takes into account the contemporary failures of the mixed economy. Yet the intellectual challenge facing social democracy is precisely that of providing convincing answers to the current ills of welfare capitalism. These authors do not address this task. Not do they confront systematically the many problems of welfare statism that have arisen over the years, including the apparent failure of redistributive and egalitarian policies, persistence of poverty, growth of professionalism and bureaucracy and the relation between economic and social welfare.

While Room acknowledges a range of shortcomings related to the practice of social welfare policy he is unable to show how these might be tackled in the context of political pluralism, market economy, and institutionalised inequalities of power and privilege of the kind that Townsend, for example, focuses on (see pp. 136-7 above). Furniss and Tilton, on the other hand, arguing from a value-committed standpoint, tend to gloss over many such criticisms levelled both from the Left and the Right. In taking Sweden as their model welfare state, and in distinguishing it as a type different from the 'social security state' such as Britain, the authors come close to taking a corporatist (IWS) view of Sweden's success.[93] For example, they stress the importance of an active labour market policy, responsible wage bargaining and the concern for efficiency in Sweden's success. But writing from a pre-crisis perspective, they fail to grasp the importance of these features in the light of the recent tribulations of welfare capitalism.

Conclusion

This chapter has been concerned with the intellectual response of the 'Centre-Left' to the current difficulties of the welfare state. The middle-of-the-road reformist tradition represented by the Centre-Left is based on practice and pragmatism rather than theoretical coherence and systematisation. A moderate collectivist wing associated with social liberalism and a Fabian socialist wing associated with social democracy were distinguished. Neither has been able to formulate a clear rationale of social welfare in a capitalist society. Both presupposes a Keynesian-style mixed economy but cannot suggest a way out of the current impasse. In recent years, some Fabians have come to recognise that the pursuit of equality through social welfare and progressive taxation has failed and that in order to create a more equal society alternative means, such as the manipulation of primary income distribution, may have to be adopted. Others realise the limits of administrative egalitarianism in the absence of appropriate popular attitudes. Writers such as Thurow and Furniss and Tilton suggest that the Centre-Left position can be articulated more systematically and given intellectual coherence. Meanwhile, Fabians must face up to the unenviable, if necessary, task of defining the limits of Fabianism clearly and deciding to work within them, however narrow they may be. Alternatively they must get down to the task of building the modern welfare state a house of theory.

6 Has the Welfare State a Future?

We began by looking at the weakened intellectual and moral legitimacy of the welfare state. The protracted crisis of the mixed economy and the apparent failure of Keynesian economics to put things right has spelled the end of the golden age of western affluence as well as of the welfare state. These changed material conditions have also spelled the break-up of the *de facto* political consensus around the mixed economy and welfare, and revived sharply the somewhat somnolent ideological conflict over the issues of welfare and economic growth. As the Centre-left position has deteriorated materially so has its (admittedly somewhat light-weight) intellectual standing. Until the mid-1970s the Centre virtually dominated the intellectual (and political) stage. The radical Right and the radical Left represented little more than fringe ideologies which did not need to be taken very seriously since they were mere echoes of the past. The 'bad old past' of free-market capitalism with its Depression and dole queues, and its antithesis Marxism with its doctrine of class war and revolution, both seemed to have been transcended in the glorious revolution of a managed market economy and Beveridgian social engineering.

The 1970s changed all that. The Centre began to lose ground rapidly and both neo-conservatives and neo-Marxists closed in. Humanity (or at least western humanity) was back to square one. If the 1950s and 1960s were intellectually (as well as politically) speaking the decade of the Centre-Left (the social democratic celebration of the middle path) the 1970s once again began to look outwards towards both ends of the ideological spectrum. What of the 1980s and beyond? It would be rash to venture a prediction. All of which goes to show how premature it is in the social sciences to celebrate the 'end' of

161

anything – whether of ideology in general, or of Marxism, or of market liberalism.

In this century history has made cruel sport of our principal intellectual paradigms – liberalism, Marxism and social democracy. For a time it has crowned each 'king' only to dethrone him later and replace him with a rival. One lesson to be learnt from history seems to be that all three – the thesis of *laisser-faire* liberalism, the antithesis of Marxist socialism, and the synthesis of social democracy – seem to be intrinsic to the social as well as spiritual (i.e. intellectual and moral) formation of modern western society. The values of individualism and liberty, whose institutional underpinning is the free market, private property and the rule of law, and the values of solidarity and community, whose institutional underpinning is common ownership, political democracy and collective services (social services), provide the essential tension which the social democratic Centre has tried to relieve, rather than resolve, through attempted reconciliation and a mix of values.

Of course, each of these major social paradigms represent much more than simply a normative position. Each includes a 'science' component which claims to show the truth, and thus to link the normative with the positive, the ends with appropriate means. Yet, as we know from the confused intellectual Odyssey of the social sciences, the search for an objective, impartial, value-free basis for social knowledge has not been successful. Never the less, since social science is ultimately a guide to action, directly or indirectly, judgements have to be made. These involve normative as well as cognitive issues. This is an important point. For an unfortunate legacy of the debate over positivism and the nature of science, and social science in particular, has been the idea of a clear divide between 'facts' and 'values'. This implies that the latter involves subjectivity and choice, while the former pertains to the realm of what 'is'. The logic of this analytic distinction is not at issue. The main point to be made is that in the social sciences at any rate (whatever the position in the natural sciences) the realm of the 'positive', the 'is', is far from unambiguous and seems destined to remain so. So many interpretations fit the observed phenomenon (itself a will-o'-the wisp) that cognitive choice (both methodological and substantive) has to be exercised all the time with only a partial grounding in reliable evidence and impeccable reasoning.

History, the temporal element, both provides a natural testing ground for large-scale social theories such as liberalism or Marxism, and also provides theories with a big escape clause, for we may claim that 'in the final analysis' – and only in the final analysis – would such and such happen. What happens in the interim is another matter. But when does the 'last instance' arrive? When do contradictions 'finally' 'mature'? How long does the interim last? All developmental hypotheses – and in the social sciences there are many – involve a long period of waiting during which we have to take the theory on trust. Conversely, many social scientific assertions of a universal nature (models, abstract theoretical propositions) are difficult to disprove with reference to facts. The result is that paradigms never die, they simply fade away – only to blossom again when history calls them to life.

Thus the 1930s belonged to Marxism, and both market liberalism and social democracy were in disarray. In the 1950s the wheel of fortune turned against Marxism and, to a lesser extent, market liberalism. Neither the atomism of *laisser-faire* nor the monism of Marxist socialism but the mix of pluralistic industrialism seemed the correct path on which at last the western societies had arrived. It was to be the finest hour of social democracy, the mixed economy and the welfare state. The nature and history of these broadly comparable paradigms show that each embodies a partial truth which gives them sufficient plausibility. In the right circumstances they give their adherents the feeling that truth – the whole or at least the large part of it – is on their side. At the moment, truth seems to have deserted the Centre in favour of the extremes of the intellectual and value spectrum.

Practical Considerations

What then of the future of the welfare state which largely represents the Centre-Left position? We shall do our best to answer this question in the light of the material presented in the earlier chapters and the sceptical position sketched above.

163

Indeed our discussion of the various perspectives, and in particular the delineation of corporatism (IWS), shows alredy where our normative and cognitive choices lie.

First, then, the normative position. Generally speaking, I believe that the Welfare State – which combines a managed market economy, a plural polity and a developed social welfare system – represents a social formation, however hybrid and compromised, worth preserving. Why? There are two reasons. First, consider the alternatives. Essentially they seem to be either a return to free market, or a socialist revolution. Let us look at each briefly.

The free-market option is currently being tried in both Britain and the United States. Its logic is economic and social *laisser-faire* (with pragmatic departures from this principle if they help the business class), a return to the Social Darwinism of Spencer. The major normative issue here is that this approach would require the relatively powerless segments of the population (workers, blacks, women) to pick up the cost of change. If progress is predicated on the survival of the fittest, then the weak must by definition be allowed to go to the wall. This approach would enhance freedom (especially of the wealthy) at the cost of social justice. It attempts to put the clock back to the 1930s. However fitfully and partially the movement for social rights (understood in the broader sense) has established a foothold in liberal market society by committing the state, the government, to certain forms of action, to taking certain measures. A return to the free market, to deregulation, amounts to a counter-revolution. It means the disestablishment of a variety of rights which do something towards maintaining minimum standards and providing a context within which the struggle against inequities can be waged. It is above all the equity claims or entitlements that are largely inscribed in the welfare state. Take, for example, the right to work, informally recognised since the 1940s. Now in some ways it is an absurdity to claim such a right within a predominantly market economy. Indeed the guarantee of full employment itself changes the nature of the economy from a free market to a regulated one. It was the genius of Keynes to show that with only minor and indirect forms of state intervention a market economy could be made to provide full

employment. And although the welfare state was more concerned with unemployment insurance, one of the assumptions
of the Beveridge Report, for example, was that the government
will try to maintain high levels of employment. In this sense the
right to work and thereby also a fully legitimate entitlement to
income has been recognised by the welfare state. The right to
education, health care and a minimum level of living are other
relevant examples. Attempts to create greater equity between
citzens – discriminated against on sexual or ethnic grounds –
through affirmative action are again measures to secure
human rights.

The neo-conservative strategy is to discredit government
and thus depoliticise, or rather desocialise, the market
economy. Yet what the politicisation of the economy from
below (full employment and the social services) has essentially
achieved is a modicum of security which a society founded on
pure market capitalism lacks and whose absence played such
havoc in the 1920s and 1930s. Thus a return to unalloyed
capitalism, even if politically feasible, without repression,
would be a return to insecurity and grosser forms of injustice.
It would be to return to a society in which basic social rights are
denied and the costs of economic change allowed to lie where
they fall. We must remember too that on all accounts technological developments and industrial restructuring of advanced capitalist economies might mean continuing large-
scale unemployment. What does a *laisser-faire* or market
economy offer in these circumstances? Even in terms of short-
term economic recovery and growth Thatcherism and
Reaganomics have little to show. At a purely technical level,
the monetary medicine applied by these pro-market regimes
has been so strong as to endanger the patient's life itself.
Inflation has been tamed and wage demands lowered at an
enormously high cost in the form of unemployment and
bankruptcies. In short the neo-conservative solution has little
to recommend either as a value-orientation, or even as a short-
term technical fix. As Thurow has pointed out, perhaps the
changes that are needed for some variant of a free market to
restore economic dynamic and growth (profits, investments,
etc.) would be so massive as to rule itself out on grounds of
equity and justice, as well as political feasibility.

What of the socialist alternative? For the other major response to the current crisis is to move toward some variant of Marxist socialism so that the contradictions of capitalism are overcome once and for all and a social system based on the recognition of human needs at last becomes a reality. In a sense, this could be the realisation of a welfare society which would take the values of welfare much further. Although attractive from this viewpoint there are several problems with this socialist vision. Normatively speaking, socialism exalts the collective over the individual, distributive justice over liberty. Moreover, in Marxist socialism, which has so far taken a more or less élitist form, the whole question of democracy remains unresolved. At any rate 'actually existing socialism' does not inspire confidence as a model to be emulated. Thus to end up with such a regime would be to jump out of the frying pan into the fire. Individualism, liberty and rule of law, of which I spoke earlier, constitute a valuable part of the modern western heritage and any progressive social system must incorporate these within itself. If it is conceded that collectivism and distributive egalitarianism are not the only desirable values then the socialist project must demonstrate that it can encompass libertarian values as well and carry forward the entire complex of values and institutions to a higher level of civilisation (as Marx for example seems to have envisaged). The problem of how to organise an efficient system of production without the use of coercion and material incentives also remains unsolved (at the level of both practice and theory). Post-revolutionary societies ('actually existing socialism') show that this could be the Achilles heel of socialism.

In short, both at the normative and technical levels, Marxist socialism, like neo-conservatism, fails to convince as a social theory of progress for advanced western societies. This does not rule out forms of transitional or gradual socialism (e.g. Eurocommunism, workers' fund socialism of Sweden) which in effect promise us that we can have our cake and eat it too. But if these have to be tried within a broadly democratic framework it remains unclear (as with Eurocommunism or the 'alternative economic strategy'[1] in Britain) how they are to realise their major objectives and how they might reconcile liberty, equality, democracy and economic growth. It may well be that historically fortunate countries (e.g. Sweden) may yet surprise us by achieving this seemingly impossible objective. But at present no one seems to have a convincing enough model of transition to democratic socialism.

If we reject neo-conservatism and Marxist socialism, then we are left with some form of Centrist position. I would like to suggest that the corporatist form of the welfare state seems to offer the possibility of overcoming some of the major defects of the post-war welfare state. Whether and to what extent corporatism might succeed is a difficult question to answer. None the less, a corporatist approach seems worth a try. Let me explain why.

First, let us note that public support for state-provided services remains high in capitalist democracies. The responsibility for maintaining full employment and general conditions of equity are also seen as the government's sphere. In this sense the welfare state shows no sign of having lost its popular appeal or legitimacy among the masses (see pp. 50-1 above). Taxation may not be popular, but right-wing expectations of Proposition 13-style tax revolts spreading throughout western countries have come to nothing. There is certainly no evidence of general support for the retrenchment of government and the privatisation of economic and social life. Admittedly, there are also some contradictory findings which suggest that conflicting tendencies may be at work (see pp. 50-1 above). But on the whole the evidence in favour of continuing support for the basic social services and the maintenance of full employment is unmistakable. As I have argued above (pp. 84-9), the victory of the Right at the polls in several countries, notably the UK and the USA, does not by any means signify the repudiation of the objectives and values of the welfare state. Rather it suggests the search for an alternative route (with some temporary hardships on the way) to roughly the same destination.

Second, the recession, the fiscal crisis and other problems of the welfare state have also shown the importance of economic welfare, of full employment and economic growth, for the masses in capitalist democracies. The key objectives seem to be security – economic and social – and prosperity. True, the influence of the media, manipulation by élites, and the sheer weight of dominant ideology have to be borne in mind.

167

However, popular surveys show that the masses do not follow blindly whatever is decreed from above – by the government of the day or by the ruling class. At least in the democracies the masses are exposed to some degree of plurality of viewpoints and beliefs and it would be well not to lose sight of the fact. In any case, as I have tried to explain earlier, my own standpoint is that the market capitalist system must meet equity claims and spread the risks and costs of social change evenly. In this sense I find my own preference for the role of government to be broadly in line with those of the masses.

If the welfare state both enjoys popular support (legitimacy) and also appears to have been effective in providing a measure of security and equity, then the next problem could be stated in the form: 'But can we afford it?' In short the problem is that of financing various services adequately and coping with the apparently negative consequence or externalities of the welfare state. Here key economic issues such as inflation, the trade-off between the economic and social wage, full employment (or some equivalent social arrangement), profitability and investment, efficiency and productivity, budget deficits, and the like have to be addressed. It is precisely the lack of an institutional framework for addressing such problems (outside electoral competition and a free-for-all interest group politics) that has brought the welfare state (DWS) into disrepute. For, as we have seen, underlying the Keynes-Beveridge model was the notion of a form of moderate collectivism that would manipulate demand to maintain employment and provide an underpinning of social security (in the wider sense) for all citizens. The assumption was that once these correctives were put in place the rest of the economy could be left, more or less, to the operation of market forces. This notion of moderate collectivism did not anticipate the possible effects of a pressure group polity on the state welfare system.

More important, the institutional separation between the 'social' (welfare) and the 'economic' (market economy) took a too static and 'social engineering' view of the social system. Social democratic reformism, typified by Richard Titmuss's approach, reinforced the idea of a sharp separation between the social (welfare and needs, etc.) and the economic (market, profits, efficiency, etc.) realms by emphasising the different values embodied in them. This emphasis had two unfortunate consequences. First, the importance of full employment and economic growth for the general welfare of the masses was obscured by the emphasis on social welfare and distribution. Second, and more important, the lack of a theoretical perspective on the social structure obscured the fact that the social and the economic were not only functionally related (interdependent) but both formed part of a larger reality (of values and institutions) of welfare capitalism. The perspective of piecemeal social intervention, based on a somewhat dramatised ethic of welfare and choice (in place of a focus on society, its dominant institutions and values), also encouraged a somewhat free-floating view of social welfare isolating it from the wider social structure of which it was a part. The connection with the social structure was chiefly made at a technical-administrative level (e.g. demography, family and household composition, urbanisation) in order to formulate needs and help with social planning. The macro-level connections with the economy and the polity (power relations, economic production, sectional interests) were on the whole missed out. The focus on the social welfare aspect of state activity has also encouraged the view in which public services, such as transport and government subsidies of various kinds to producers and consumers, were seen as lying outside the sphere of the welfare state. The upshot was that social policies were seen as unrelated not only to economic policies but to public policies as well. This may have been especially true of Britain, but a similar institutional separation in the analysis of these various sectors can be seen in other English-speaking countries.

The isolation of the social from the economic, of social welfare activities from other relevant activities of the state (e.g. subsidies, employment policy), has also inhibited the search for appropriate institutional forms through which the problem of interdependence among these spheres, especially between economic and social welfare, might be addressed. There is an important difference here between countries like Sweden with its Labour Market Board and centralised wage bargaining and Austria with its social partnership institutions on the one hand, and say Britain or Canada on the other. The corporatism of countries like Austria and Sweden, whatever its shortcomings, at least in principle takes the social services and social welfare out of the 'ghetto' and tends to relate them to the wider institutional and group context of society. It is due to the ability of countries like Sweden to address the problems of productivity, wage settlements, inflation and technological change through institutions which seek to arrive at a working consensus (consensus, as we saw above, has been stressed far more and quite explicitly in Austria) that potentially adverse economic consequences of full employment, wage militancy and rising public expenditure have been avoided for a long period. It should also be remembered that there is a good deal of voluntarism involved in wage bargaining as well as other forms of social co-operation between employers and trade unions in these countries. Corporatism, in short, must not be equated with the extension of government.

The class relationships and interests involved in corporatist arrangements are bound to vary from one country to another. But it would be idle to pretend, as Marxists tend to do, that all such arrangements are a way of subordinating labour to capital's interests. This may be the case in countries where labour is weak organisationally and ideologically. And that is why corporatist policies (meaning usually a one-sided imposition of wage control by the government) are normally rejected by unions in such countries in the absence of a *quid pro quo* in the form of social contract. Yet, as the example of Britain shows, free collective bargaining may be good for labour in the short run (or rather for those sections of the labour force in a strong position to drive a bargain) but in the long run the price paid for waging a class war (i.e. wage struggle) can be high in terms of mass unemployment, economic decline and inadequate social services. Britain's case also amply demonstrates that wage militancy has nothing to do with class consciousness and socialism in the Marxist sense. In the absence of socialist consciousness and an effective strategy of revolution, a free-for-all can only benefit the Right. Corporatist arrangements on the other hand have the merit of extending the notion of collective responsibility for system maintenance by involving those with most economic power in collective decision-making. In this sense corporatism (IWS) carries the logic of the welfare state (DWS) a step further. It helps realise, in some small measure, the idea of 'planning' in the context of a mixed economy and plural polity.

Corporatism, it is true, involves the centralisation of the decision-making process and entails by-passing parliament to some extent, in so far as important decisions are made outside it. But it must be remembered that in the Welfare State decisions are being made outside parliament in any case (e.g. investment and pricing decisions by corporations, collective agreements between groups of workers and companies). Thus what is involved in corporatism is more the coordination and harmonisation of certain kinds of decisions rather than their removal from the parliamentary arena. Indeed corporatism adds a measure of social accountability by making certain kinds of decision-making and their underlying rationale more visible and public. It must also be remembered that what is involved primarily is a broad framework of understanding between major economic groupings regarding economic growth, wages, prices, inflation and similar economic issues. This still leaves a very large area of economic, social and political issues to be debated and decided upon through the normal political processes. True, some measure of central-isation in decision-making by major economic associations, including the state, is the essence of this approach. Given certain national objectives (economic and social) a measure of co-operation, consensus and stability seem necessary. Hence a measure of centralisation. Moreover, if the economic and social aspects of welfare are to be connected properly at the macro-level some degree of 'planning' becomes inevitable. Hence too centralisation. But general decisions about wages, prices and investment still leave plenty of room for pluralism within a broad framework of national consensus.

It is also important to remind ourselves of the limits – or rather the limitations – of the corporate welfare state (IWS). Like the welfare state (DWS) it cannot be a means to socialism, to an egalitarian society. As we have seen, the social demo-cratic hopes of changing the nature of income distribution through a sharply progressive system of taxation and free social services have not been realised. Thirty years of welfare statism and a mountain of research into this area seem to show that such expectations were misplaced and are unlikely to be realised. The pursuit of equality (i.e. equality of rewards and outcome rather than equality of consideration) must take other forms. Other, perhaps more direct methods of intervention may have to be devised and put into practice. Social welfare as Marshall, Beveridge and other moderate collectivists have always pointed out, is primarily a means to social security and citizenship rights. No doubt, social insurance itself, as well as equity claims generally, involve greater equality of consideration and also quality of opportunity. But these measures have little to do with equality of outcome *per se*.

It will be remembered that, in the case of Austria at least, there was a tacit understanding that the respective shares of capital and labour are not a subject of bargaining and that the social consensus was based on the recognition of this point. In Sweden, on the other hand, there has been no such understanding and presumably the search for greater equality through the policy of wage solidarity and through the welfare state more generally has been active. However in Sweden too the tripartite (or bipartite) deliberations do not seem to have been concerned with a planned reduction in social (including income) inequality. Nor do data on the distribution of income and wealth show such reduction in equality. The corporatist welfare state, rather like its predecessor, is not much concerned with equality. Rather it is concerned with enhancing economc and social welfare simultaneously (what a corporatist Mao Tse Tung might have called 'walking on two legs') and ensuring that national minima are maintained and improved. This is not to say that the pursuit of equality (in its various aspects) cannot be carried on in conjunction with the structures and institutions of welfare. But it must be borne in mind that that objective is extraneous to the corporatist welfare state (IWS).

But how does the IWS relate to the normative issues surrounding state intervention? A major issue raised by the neo-conservatives, as well as Marxists like O'Connor and Offe, is the use of the state by a variety of particularistic interests which results in an unprincipled growth of the state budget and the state sector. Substantially the same question has been raised by others (e.g. Bell and Hirsch) in pointing out that the public sector has tended to become more an arena in which claims and counter-claims are made than a community with some form of social morality to underpin collective action. Can the IWS address this problem? I believe it can, even if indirectly. The co-operation of major economic groups with the government in looking at the economic picture as a whole (including economic and social welfare) is helpful in moderating un-principled government growth. In any case, because of the compartmentalisation of economic, social and public policies, the welfare state has tended to be seen narrowly in terms of social policy alone. Government's wider economic activity (e.g. aid to industry, agriculture and other sectors through subsidies, fiscal policy) is often left out of the picture. The corporatist approach would be able to take a broader view of the consequences of government action. This across-the-board view of state welfare activity may promote a more rational and principled approach to policy. At any rate, the idea of something like a public interest is more likely to be addressed through co-operation and consensus (as, for example, during the 'Social Contract' between the Labour government and the trade unions in Britain) than under the free-for-all pattern typical of the pluralist welfare state (DWS).

On the other hand, *pace* moderate collectivists such as Marshall and Robson, it would be more rather than less difficult under a corporatist regime to differentiate clearly something called the welfare state from the rest of the state's activities. The idea that a state welfare sector – communally oriented, based on normative consensus and with clearly defined objectives – can co-exist with competition and conflict in a plural society appears unrealistic. Indeed, one should recognise clearly that interest-group politics and government are arenas of competition, and that a variety of claims and counter-claims – both material and ideological – will continue to be made. Economic and social welfare will therefore have to be understood in a wider sense and we shall still have to ask of specific state activities as to whose welfare they are serving and in accordance with what values or principles.

Indeed it may be premature, if not unrealistic, to think of defining the nature of government activity (distributional or otherwise) in normative terms. What the IWS seems to promise is a measure of working consensus over the system of mixed economy and state-protected minimum standards. Beyond that lies the realm of pluralism, of values and of interests. Short of authoritarianism, whether of the Right or the Left, or some miracle it is difficult to see how one can have a modern society without conflict. But this need not rule out some measure of consensus and accommodation among key social groups in order to sustain better those conditions in which a wide variety of conflicts can continue without causing serious dysfunctions. It would be absurd to pretend that some form of corporatism can be a panacea for the ills of modern society in general, and welfare capitalism in particular. But it seems to offer an institutional framework, in the context of a capitalist economy and liberal polity, within which the values of the welfare state (DWS) may be better realised.

To argue in favour of corporatism is one thing: to demonstrate its political feasibility is quite another. The political question is important but too large an issue to be explored here. Moreover, the question of political action can be considered meaningfully only in relation to a particular country and its economic and political conditions. Generally speaking those political groupings and forces that lend most support to the welfare state (social democracy and the labour movement) are also the natural constituency for the IWS (remember that we have been speaking throughout of democratic forms of corporatism). The main issue seems to be to win back the ideological initiative from the Right by pointing to the model of an advanced welfare capitalism (IWS) as a realistic and evolutionary alternative. As regards the political feasibility of corporatism in a particular country, the nature of capital, working-class organisation and ideology, level of union membership, political structure and traditions are among some of the more important influences (see pp. 108-9 above). Indeed, it is best to see the IWS as *one* possible (and potentially successful) response to the current crisis among others. It may not suit all countries and diversity of national solutions and responses may not be a bad thing after all, provided it is based on popular consent.

Theoretical Considerations

It is likely that those of us who live under welfare capitalism of one sort or another will continue to live in similar regimes in the foreseeable future. The Right is unlikely to succeed in winding down the welfare state and returning us to the pristine state of *laisser-faire* capitalism. (Right-wing authoritarianism cannot however be ruled out.) The Left is equally unlikely to usher in a really socialist regime which would spell the end of welfare capitalism. That being the case we need to understand this hybrid of democratic-welfare-capitalism as best we can. In this task of comprehension the insights of the various intellectual orientations examined in the earlier chapters can be used selectively without, as it were, having to throw in one's lot with any one of them. This is the position adopted here. And it seems to fit the normative position outlined above, which is something of the order of Centre-Left. From such a vantage point one can look at both extremes and perhaps borrow from them whatever suits one's analytical and normative purpose. Clearly, it would help a great deal if a new Marx or Keynes were to appear and so dazzle us with his (her?) brilliance that we drop our ifs and buts and follow wherever he (she?) decrees. But what happens in the meanwhile? We have to make the most of the legacy bequeathed us by post-war social science to find our way through the unsure terrain in which we find ourselves at the moment.

One thing is clear, facile sociological theories of modernisation, industrialism and convergence, piecemeal social engineering and interventionism stand discredited to a greater or lesser extent. New orientations are needed. Not, let us be clear, because some new approach will finally (!) reveal the truth to us but simply because social thought – or social science if it is preferred – is a part of our attempt to comprehend and to act on the basis of that comprehension. However unreliable a guide social thought may be we cannot do without it. Whether we like it or not, judgements have to be made and decisions arrived at. And it is better to make these in terms of ideas and beliefs that are explicit, coherent and open to public scrutiny. That, in short, is what social theory is about. But what kind of theory? Let me outline the position briefly.

Social expenditure and social welfare institutions, on a scale on which they now exist in western countries, are a post-war phenomenon unprecedented in western history. Their relationship with the rest of the social structure, in particular the interaction between the economy, the polity and the welfare sector, needs to be understood far more adequately than is the case at present. Some form of a sociology (or, if it is preferred, political economy) of the welfare state is needed to underpin the practical, social problem focused studies of welfare. The latter have largely served the function of handmaiden to the welfare state. More often than not this social engineering approach has been concerned with theories and concepts related to the practice of social welfare. What we also need is a structural analysis of the welfare state. Not simply forms of social analysis *for* the welfare state but also social analysis *of* the welfare state seen as a part of the social system. In order to do this adequately, something along these lines seems to me to be necessary.

First, it is necessary to specify the nature of western economies clearly. It is no use pretending, for example, that capitalism does not exist and what we have is an industrial or post-industrial economy. This way of conflating the economy with the level of technology so that the distinctive features of the former disappear will simply not do. Nor will it do to take capitalist market economy entirely for granted and thus assume it out of the analysis as the social administration approach has often tended to do. What is of particular importance is to recognise capitalism as a system of production (and not just distribution) with all its 'virtues' and 'vices'. For there is a strong tendency among Left Fabians and others to see capitalism, when it is so identified, as largely a system of property and class privilege – in short as a structure of distribution of life-chances. This tendency to isolate the social (i.e. distribution) from the economic (i.e. production) must be overcome if the nature of welfare capitalism is to be understood properly.

Secondly, a systemic approach to the analysis of the welfare state must be adopted. In short, reformism and piecemeal social engineering must be situated within the context of a social system. This would allow us to explore the relationship between the institution of social welfare and the other major institutional orders (e.g. the market economy and the plural polity). The relationship between the economic and the social (e.g. wages, employment, social expenditure, subsidy) could thus be explored systematically. Institutions would be analysed both in terms of their value implications as well as functional (or dysfunctional) implications for other institutions. Above all, the 'parts' (e.g. the institutions of welfare) must be seen in relation to some conception of the social structure as a 'whole' (e.g. the social system of welfare capitalism).

Third, and this is related to the previous point, the analysis of social policy needs to straddle the institutional and group perspectives. In an unrecognised, *ad hoc* way policy analysis does utilise both these perspectives. But the connection between these two aspects of social reality – between system and social integration – and its importance needs to be grasped more firmly and incorporated into analysis more explicitly. It is of course the Marxist perspective on the welfare state that recognises the relationship between the institutional contradictions of capitalism (e.g. declining profits) and the class struggle (e.g. full employment and wage militancy) most clearly. The corporatist approach, in a sense, turns Marxism on its head in recognising that in order to integrate the institutional level successfully (social welfare and market economy), it is necessary to harmonise group relationships (some degree of working consensus between workers and employers). Seen from another angle, to combine the institutional and group levels of analysis is to emphasise that the welfare state is both about functions (providing services, meeting needs, etc.) as well as group interests and conflicts. It has become increasingly clear that the study of social welfare institutions (e.g the National Health Service) cannot be isolated from the study of bureaucracy and the professions (e.g. the doctors) as interest groups.

Finally, those of us who live in the English-speaking world need to look at the countries of Western Europe, notably Sweden and Austria, rather more closely than we have done in the past. At the close of the nineteenth century, English-speaking countries, (Britain, and to a lesser extent the United States) had turned increasingly to the Bismarckian welfare state of Germany (Lloyd George's insurance scheme was largely inspired by the German example) to add a social dimension to *laisser-faire* capitalism. Indeed, while jealous of their national traditions and institutions western countries have also borrowed freely from each other and adapted 'foreign' elements to suit domestic circumstances. After a long interlude in which the Keynes-Beveridge model (the latter element somewhat modified) seemed adequate for welfare capitaism the time seems to have come once again for shopping around in the market place of ideas and institutions.

Post-war Britain, which used to be a positive model of the welfare state, at least for English-speaking countries, has increasingly turned into its very opposite. Britain's steady economic decline, her relative decline as a welfare spender (though the National Health Service may be providing good value for money) and her inability to solve economic and institutional problems has made the British welfare state appear increasingly unimaginative, uninnovative and on the defensive. It has proved an easy target of the Right which has used it as a scapegoat for most, if not all, of Britain's ills.

Fabian reformism with its method of piecemeal social engineering (unlike the holistic approach more prevalent in Western Europe) has tended to isolate social welfare and its study from the wider structures of society. Moreover, reformist concerns have not been conducive to cross-national analysis. In the coming years therefore cross-national studies focused on the institutions and practices (at the macro- or societal level) of relevant European as well as English-speaking countries need to be developed.

True, perceptive students of British political economy have been looking at Europe for several decades now. British membership of the EEC has also encouraged cross-national studies of poverty, and the like. None the less, the current impasse of welfare capitalism and the 'ascendancy' of neo-conservatism in Britain and the United States, the two major English speaking countries, makes it an urgent task to look for ways of responding to the crisis other than monetarism and orthodox labourism. For one thing is certain: Keynes is dead and we now live in the post-Keynesian era. Marx, it is true, is alive and well but it appears cannot help – at least not much. There is of course the 'science' of muddling through.

Notes and References

Chapter 1

1 Hayek (1944); Friedman (1962).
2 Conservative Political Centre (1958: 9).
3 Titmuss (1962: 15-17).
4 Titmuss (1962); Townsend (1962); Kolko (1962); Harrington (1962).
5 Galbraith (1958); Harrington (1962).
6 Titmuss (1962).
7 Abel-Smith and Townsend (1965); US House Committee on Education and Labor, 'Poverty in the United States' in Meissner (1966: 43-68).
8 Guest (1980: chs 9, 10); Armitage (1975: 217-18); Leiby (1978: chs 15, 16); Grønbjerg (1977: ch. 8).
9 Wilensky (1965: xviii, li).
10 Marcuse (1968: 52-3); Baran and Sweezy (1968: chs 6, 7).
11 Rimlinger (1971: 163-6, 177-8).
12 ibid. pp.151, 222; Weaver (1950: 201, 206).
13 Marshall (1965: 180-1).
14 ibid., p.97.
15 ibid.
16 Grønbjerg (1978: 60); Marris and Rein (1974).
17 George and Wilding (1976: 46-52).
18 Beveridge Report (1942); Marshall (1965: 78-80).
19 George and Wilding (1976: ch. 3).
20 Aubrey Jones, 'Inflation as an Industrial Problem', in Skidelsky (ed.) (1977: 53).
21 George and Wilding (1976: ch. 3).
22 Richard M. Titmuss, 'The Welfare State: Images and Realities', in Schottland (ed.) (1967: 100-1); Marshall (1965: 75-6, 88).
23 Parsons (1951); Mishra (1981: 50-5).
24 Mishra (1981: chs 3, 4); Kumar (1978: 57, 149-54).
25 See e.g. Smith (1973: ch. 2); Kerr et al. (1973).
26 Kerr et al. (1973).

27 Mishra (1981: ch. 3).
28 Mishra (1973); Williamson and Flemming (1977); Weed (1979).
29 See e.g. Crosland (1964; chs I, II); Dahrendorf (1959: ch. II); Robin Blackburn, 'The New Capitalism', in Blackburn (ed.) (1972: 164-86).
30 Parsons (1971: 20-2); Lipset (1969: 406); Dahrendorf (1959: 62).
31 Mishra (1981: 29).
32 Titmuss (1968: 14).
33 Reisman (1977: 35, 163-9).
34 Gough (1979: 32-8, 49-54).
35 O'Connor (1973).
36 Moynihan (1965: 10-11); Winch (1972: chs 13, 14).
37 Moynihan (1965: 6, 10-11).
38 See below pp. 31-3, 39.
39 Weber (1930).
40 Popper (1961: 64).
41 ibid.
42 ibid., p. 67.
43 Hayek (1944).
44 Popper (1957: 125).
45 Crosland (1964: 79).
46 ibid.
47 ibid., chs II, IV.
48 George and Wilding (1976: 82-4).
49 ibid., ch. 4; Tawney (1966: chs 10, 11).
50 George and Wilding (1976: 69-75).
51 Skidelsky (ed.) (1977).
52 See e.g. Gouldner (1971); Frank (1970); Giddens (1973: 13-22).
53 See e.g. Goldthorpe (1964); Weinberg (1969); Mishra (1976).
54 See e.g. J. H. Westergaard, 'Sociology: The Myth of Classlessness'; and Robin Blackburn 'The New Capitalism', in Blackburn (ed.) (1972: 119-63, 164-86).
55 Kumar (1978: ch. 8); Bell (1976); Kaldor (1979).
56 Friedman and Friedman (1980); Skidelsky (1977).
57 See e.g. Bottomore (ed.) (1975); Willer and Willer (1973); Habermas (1971); Rex (1974).
58 Crosland (1964).
59 Saville (1957-8).
60 See e.g. Titmuss (1962: 187-8).
61 Townsend and Bosanquet, 'Introduction', and Townsend, 'Social Planning and The Control of Priorities', in Townsend and Bosanquet (eds) (1972: 5-11, 274-300).
62 Parkin (1971: 117-19); Castles (1978: 87-9).

63 Miliband (1973); Poulantzas (1973).
64 Miliband (1973: chs 4, 9).
65 Blackburn (1967: 14-15; Roby (ed.) (1974).
66 See e.g. McIntosh (1981: 32-42); Rose and Rose (1982: 8, 14-18).

Chapter 2

1 George and Wilding (1976: ch. 2).
2 Titmuss (1974: 30-1).
3 Friedman and Friedman (1980: 331).
4 Steinfels (1979).
5 Centre for Policy Studies (1975: 11-13).
6 See pp. 75-6 below.
7 Kristol (1978: 247).
8 King (1975: 286).
9 ibid., p. 287.
10 See e.g. Brittan (1977: 249-51).
11 ibid., pp. 255-7.
12 ibid., p. 251.
13 Downs (1957: 96).
14 Hayek (1973: 10).
15 ibid., pp. 9-10.
16 Niskanen (1971: 38-40).
17 Friedman and Friedman (1980: 343).
18 ibid., p. 125.
19 Brittan (1977: 242-3).
20 Friedman and Friedman (1980: 124).
21 Quoted in Steinfels (1979: 221).
22 Quoted in Steinfels (1979: 220).
23 ibid.
24 Kristol (1978: 247).
25 King (1975: 285).
26 Friedman (1977: 7).
27 Quoted in Wildavsky (1980: 21).
28 ibid., p. 22.
29 ibid., p. 24.
30 Irving Kristol, 'Welfare: The Best of Intentions, The Worst of Results', in Weinberger (ed.) (1974: 241).
31 ibid.
32 Gilder (1982: 13).
33 ibid., p. 150.
34 ibid., p. 144.

35 Gans (1972).
36 Nathan Glazer, 'The Limits of Social Policy', in Weinberger (ed.) (1974: 256).
37 ibid.
38 ibid, p. 257.
39 See e.g. Friedman and Friedman (1980: 340-5).
40 See e.g. Silverman (1970: chs 3, 6); Rex, 'Social Structure and Humanistic Sociology', in Rex (ed.) (1974a: 187-204).
41 Friedman and Friedman (1980: 24).
42 See e.g. Rudolf Klein, 'Values Power and Policies', in OECD (1981: 171).
43 Crozier *et al.* (1975).
44 ibid.
45 ibid., p. 164.
46 ibid.
47 Brittan (1977: 255).
48 See e.g. Goldthorpe, 'The Current Inflation: Towards a Sociological Account', in Hirsch and Goldthorpe (eds) (1978: 196-9).
49 Brittan (1977: 267).
50 Douglas (1976: 493-5).
51 King (1975: 293).
52 Nathan Glazer, 'The Limits of Social Policy', in Weinberger (ed.) (1974: 258).
53 ibid.
54 Daniel P. Moynihan, 'The Professors and the Poor', in Weinberger (ed.) (1974: 135-7, 146); Moynihan (1973: 3-4).
55 Hayek (1978: 34).
56 ibid.
57 Friedman (1977: 35).
58 Hayek (1944: 36).
59 ibid.
60 ibid., p. 37.
61 King (1975: 296).
62 See e.g. Hayek (1973: 14).
63 See e.g. Buchanan and Wagner (1977: 93); Friedman and Friedman (1980: 309-12).
64 Buchanan and Wagner (1977: 3-4).
65 ibid., p. 94.
66 ibid., pp. 96-9.
67 ibid., ch. 12.
68 See e.g. Gilder (1982).
69 The so-called 'Laffer curve' suggests such relationships; ibid., ch. 15.

70 See e.g. Buchanan and Wagner (1977: 163).
71 Friedman and Friedman (1980: 348-55).
72 See Peretz (1982); Bennet and DiLorenzo (1982).
73 Danziger (1980).
74 See e.g. Jones (1980: 145-6).
75 See e.g. 'Tory Manifesto', *The Economist* (14 April, 1979, p. 2); 'Election Profile: Margaret Thatcher', *The Economist* (21 April 1979, pp. 39-42); The Policies of the Parties', *New Society* (19 April 1979: 142-4).
76 Jones (1980: 155-7); Lewis and Harrison (1981: 46-51).
77 *Manchester Guardian Weekly* (31 January 1982: 3); (2 May 1982: 5).
78 Gough (1979: 128).
79 Walker (1980: 47-51); Stein *et al.* (1982: 46-54).
80 Gough (1979: 142); Navarro (1982: 56-7); Davis (1981: 45-9).
81 See e.g. 'CBI Warns The Government' *Manchester Guardian Weekly* (29 August 1982: 3).
82 On e.g. medical care, see 'Going Private: The Case Against Private Medicine', *Critical Social Policy* (1982: 79-89); *Manchester Guardian Weekly* (6 December 1981: 3).
83 Gough (1979: 73); Mishra (1981: 116-17).
84 On these questions, see e.g. 'Reagan's Big Gamble', *Newsweek* (8 February 1982: 24-34); 'President's Tax Increase Provokes Storm', *Manchester Guardian Weekly* (22 August 1982: 15).
85 Alvin Schorr, 'The Coast to Coast Soup Line', *Manchester Guardian Weekly* (24 January 1982: 9).
86 ibid; Rayner (1982: 90-8).
87 *Manchester Guardian Weekly* (1 May 1983: 9); (22 May 1983: 7).
88 'A Business Boss's Plea for the Poor', *Manchester Guardian Weekly* (20 December 1981: 16).
89 Everett Carll Ladd, Jr and Seymour Martin Lipset, 'Public Opinion and Public Policy', in Duignan and Rabushka (eds) (1980: 68-72); *Newsweek* (8 February 1982: 34); *New Society* 4 October 1979: 12-13; 20 March 1980: 606).
90 See e.g. Gough (1979: 82-4).
91 See n. 89.
92 Harold L. Wilensky, 'Democratic Corporatism, Consensus, and Social Policy', in OECD (1981: 193); Phillips (1982: 127); Peretz (1982: 231-49).
93 *Manchester Guardian Weekly* (17 October 1982: 15; 2 January 1983: 15, 16).
94 Douglas (1981: 183).
95 See nn. 85, 86.

96 OECD (1976); (1977); (1978). See also Gough (1979: 84-8).
97 See e.g. Thurow (1981: 74).
98 OECD (1978: 39-40).
99 ibid.
100 Friedman and Friedman (1980: 129).
101 OECD (1982a: 8, 62 and 'Basic Statistics: International Comparisons'); OECD (1982: 28); Lester C. Thurow, 'Equity, Efficiency, Social Justice and Redistribution', in Stoffaës (ed.) (1982: 323).
102 Kristol (1978: 243).
103 On growth rates, see Matthews *et al.* (1982: 498); Shonfield (1969: 4).
104 King (1975; 285).
105 ibid.
106 Steinfels (1979: 223-4).
107 Wildavsky (1980: 23).
108 Horowitz, in Horowtiz (ed.) (1979: 233).
109 ibid.
110 Melvin M. Webber, 'A Difference Paradigm for Planning', in Burchell and Sternlieb (eds) (1978: 157).
111 ibid., p. 156.
112 Wildavsky (1980: 23).
113 Reisman (1977: 9, 28).
114 Hayek (1978: 13).
115 ibid., p. 16.
116 Jessop (1977: 368-9).
117 George and Wilding (1976: ch. 2).
118 Durkheim (1964: 200-29); Mishra (1981: 51-2).
119 Titmuss (1963: 75-87).
120 Hayek (1976: 115).
121 ibid., pp. 68-71.
122 See e.g. Rawls (1971: ch. I).
123 Hayek (1976: 62-5).
124 Friedman and Friedman (1980: 13).
125 Gough (1979: x).

Chapter 3

1 Mandel (1968: 13).
2 ibid., p. 15.
3 Baran and Sweezy (1968: 17).
4 Miliband (1973) and Poulantzas (1973) were the outstanding

works. Poulantzas's work, first published in France in 1968, was translated into English in 1973.

5 See e.g. Holloway and Picciotto (eds) (1978).
6 See e.g. Saville (1957-8); Miliband (1968: 10-12); Blackburn (1967: 10-14).
7 Miliband (1973: ch. 9); Blackburn (1967: 15); Poulantzas (1973).
8 Althusser and Balibar (1970) was first published in France in 1968.
9 See e.g. Mandel (1968: 337-8, 529-30); Althusser (1971: 123-49); Poulantzas (1975: 25).
10 See e.g. O'Connor (1973); Habermas (1976); Gamble and Walton (1976); Gough (1979); Frank (1980).
11 Gough (1979: 152).
12 O'Connor (1973: 1-10).
13 Gamble and Walton (1976: 146).
14 O'Connor (1973: 7).
15 Gough (1979: 69-72).
16 ibid., p. 56.
17 ibid., pp. 11-14; Gamble and Walton (1976: 162-74). For a non-economic perspective on crisis tendencies, see Habermas (1976).
18 Gough (1979: 14-15); Gamble and Walton (1976: ch. 5).
19 O'Connor (1973: 9).
20 ibid.
21 See e.g. O'Connor (1981: 44-7).
22 Shonfield (1969: 178, 192-3); King (1973: 291-313).
23 Extreme caution is needed in applying the notions of profit and loss to public enterprises. On this and related points, see e.g. Richard Pryke, 'Public Enterprise in Practice: The British Experience of Nationalization During the Past Decade'; and Pierre Dreyfus, 'The Efficiency of Public Enterprise: Lessons of the French Experience', in Baumol (ed.) (1980).
24 O'Connor (1973: 1).
25 ibid.
26 ibid., p. 9.
27 ibid.
28 ibid., p. 2.
29 ibid.
30 ibid., p. 67.
31 ibid.
32 ibid.
33 The Planning-Programming-Budgeting System (PPBS) was imported into the civilian government in the US from the Department of Defense. It was meant to facilitate 'rational' choice

among policy and programme alternatives on the basis of explicit criteria and firm cost and performance data. The system became compulsory throughout the government in 1965. It proved impractical (essentially because of its political and value-neutral assumptions) and was quietly abandoned in 1971. See Anderson (1979: 164). See Hoos (1972: 64-77) for a critical appraisal of PPBS.

34 O'Connor (1973: 9-10).
35 Gough (1979: 127).
36 Gamble and Walton (1976: 172).
37 Gough (1979; ch. 6).
38 See e.g. Gamble and Walton (1976: 18-33); Frank (1980: 50-4).
39 Gamble and Walton (1976: 192).
40 ibid., p. 32.
41 Frank (1980: 137).
42 ibid., pp. 137-9.
43 Gough (1979: 151).
44 ibid., p. 14.
45 Gough (1975: 89).
46 ibid., p. 92.
47 Habermas (1979: 78).
48 Rustin (1980: 72).
49 Hall (1979: 17-18).
50 ibid.
51 Corrigan (1979: 15).
52 ibid., p. 14.
53 See n. 89, ch. 2.
54 Jones (1980: 156).
55 On increased rates of tax burden on households, see OECD (1978: 39-58).
56 See e.g. Wolfe (1981: 12-13).
57 Davis (1981: 44).
58 Jones (1980: 145-6). See also n. 75, ch. 2.
59 Wolfe (1981: 15).
60 ibid.
61 Gough (1979: 153).
62 ibid.
63 ibid.
64 Gough (1979: 146-51).
65 Taylor-Gooby and Dale (1981: 264).
66 Wilson (1980: 87).
67 ibid.
68 Taylor-Gooby and Dale (1981: 185).

69 Ginsburg (1979: 11).
70 See e.g. Gosden (1973: 46); Bruce (1965: 149); Mishra (1981: 116-17).
71 Bruce (1965: 148-9).
72 Gough (1979: 122-4); Ginsburg (1979: 9-13).
73 O'Connor (1973: 246).
74 Westergaard and Resler (1976: 178).
75 Gough (1979: 141).
76 ibid., p. 143.
77 ibid., p. 142.
78 See however Union for Radical Political Economics (1981), esp. parts IV and V, for a Marxist analysis of public employment.
79 On contradictions and conflict in socialist societies, see e.g. Mao Tse Tung (1967); Parkin (1972); Lane (1976).
80 Although socialist societies on the whole provide full employment and a wide range of social benefits they do so within the context of a totalitarian political order. On the 'contradictory' nature of socialism in these societies, see George and Manning (1980); Lane (1976); Mishra (1981: 155-7).
81 Frank (1980: 151-2).

Chapter 4

1 Schmitter, 'Introduction'; and 'Still the Century of Corporatism?', in Schmitter and lehmbruch (eds) (1979: 4, 7-52).
2 For example Wilensky (1976); Janowitz (1976).
3 For the distinction between these two types of integration, see Mishra (1981: 54) and (1982). Very briefly, system integration refers to integration of a functional nature between institutions, and social integration to integration of a relational nature between groups.
4 See p. 171 below.
5 See Schmitter, 'Introduction'; and Lehmbruch 'Consociational Democracy, Class Conflict and the New Corporatism', and 'Liberal Corporatism and Party Government', in Schmitter and Lehmbruch (eds) (1979: 4-5, 54-5, 147-84). See also n. 1.
6 On Germany and Italy, see e.g. Richardson (1975: ch. 6). On Japan, see T. J. Pempel and Keiichi Tsunekawa 'Corporatism Without Labor? The Japanese Anomaly', in Schmitter and Lehmbruch (eds) (1979: 231-70).
7 The question of the state-society relationship in its various ramifications, including the relationship between public employ-

ment and welfare policies and party political patronage, though important, is much too large a subject to be broached here. Suffice to say that the shift from the DWS to the IWS politicises the economy rather more, but there are no other obvious implications for the relationship between the economy, polity and welfare.

8 See Dorfman (1979: 2-3, 66-87, 107-11); Smith (1979: 149-53, 165-71).
9 OECD (1980: 33-5, 37-43).
10 See Lehmbruch, 'Consociational Democracy, Class Conflict and the New Corporatism', and 'Liberal Corporatism and Party Government'; Birgitta Nedelmann and Kurt G. Meir, 'Theories of Contemporary Corporatism: Static or Dynamic', in Schmitter and Lehmbruch (eds) (1979: 55-9, 108-18, 157).
11 Robert H. Salisbury, 'Why No Corporatism in America?', in Schmitter and Lehmbruch (eds) (1979: 228).
12 Russo, 'Il Compromesso Storico: The Italian Communist Party from 1968 to 1978', in Filo Della Torre *et al.* (eds) (1979: 78-80); 'Berlinguer: Socialism Based on Democracy', *Manchester Guardian Weekly* (25 April 1982: 12).
13 OECD (1982: 28-30), (1981a: 23).
14 OECD (1982: 22, 28-30), (1981b: 51).
15 OECD (1982: 47), (1981a: 23).
16 On the development of social partnership in Austria, see OECD (1981a: 29-40).
17 On these and other points mentioned above, see OECD (1981a).
18 OECD (1981a: 33).
19 ibid., pp. 31-2, 160, 185.
20 OECD (1982: 47).
21 Loew (1980: 70, 79); OECD (1982: 48-9), (1981a: 158).
22 Jones (1976: 16-17); Shonfield (1969: 201).
23 Jones (1976: 63-4); Shonfield (1969: 200-1).
24 Jones (1976: 18-22).
25 ibid., pp. 79-80; OECD (1981c: 35).
26 OECD (1981c: 35).
27 ibid., pp. 5, 47-8.
28 OECD (1982a: 35-7, 43, 50).
29 OECD (1981c: 5, 45-7).
30 *The Economist* (16 October 1982: 68); *Sweden Now* (1982: 3-4, 16 (5)).
31 Gamble and Walton (1976: 152-8).

Chapter 5

1 Donnison (1979: 147).
2 See nn. 74 and 75 ch. 2. See also 'For Whose Benefit?', *New Society* (26 April 1979: 183).
3 See e.g. Davis (1981: 44).
4 Rustin (1980: 71).
5 Crosland (1964).
6 See e.g. Meacher (1982).
7 See e.g. Titmuss (1973).
8 See e.g. Pinker (1971); George and Wilding (1976); Mishra (1981).
9 Robson (1976: 7).
10 ibid., p. 36.
11 ibid., p. 41.
12 ibid., p. 15.
13 Janowitz (1976).
14 Bell (1979: 249).
15 ibid., p. 256.
16 ibid., p. 281.
17 Hirsch (1977).
18 ibid., p. 190.
19 Wilding (1976: 149).
20 See Reisman (1977) for an appraisal of Titmuss.
21 See especially 'Citizenship and Social Class', in Marshall (1963).
22 Marshall (1981: 104-36.).
23 ibid., pp. 124-5, 129.
24 ibid., pp. 130-2.
25 See Mishra (1982: 105-7).
26 Marshall (1981: 129).
27 Furniss and Tilton (1979: 23-4).
28 ibid., p. 24.
29 The redistribution involved is very largely horizontal (concerning life-cycle transfer of resources) rather than vertical. See, for example, Webb and Sieve (1971); Wilensky (1975: ch. 5); Mishra (1981: 120-1).
30 Townsend (1979: 894).
31 Le Grand (1982: 137).
32 ibid., p. 142.
33 For the views of R. H. Tawney and T. H. Marshall, for example, see Johnson (1972: 12-14).
34 See e.g. Johnson (1972).
35 Townsend (1980: 100).

36 Field (1981).
37 ibid., p. 15.
38 Field (1981).
39 Townsend (1979: 924).
40 On Townsend's definition of poverty (based on the resources necessary to maintain the norms and standards prevalent in the community) nearly a quarter of the British population was poor in the late 1960s (ibid., p. 895).
41 ibid., p. 926.
42 Townsend (1980: 103).
43 ibid., p. 106.
44 See e.g. Field (1981: 21).
45 Townsend (1980: 106).
46 Le Grand (1982: 150-1).
47 Field (1981: 214).
48 Meacher (1982: 245).
49 See Marshall (1981: 123-36).
50 ibid., p. 135.
51 ibid., pp. 124-5, 129-33.
52 ibid., p. 117.
53 ibid.
54 Robson (1976: 35-6, 45-6, 75).
55 ibid., p. 58.
56 ibid., pp. 174-5.
57 Pinker (1979).
58 See e.g. Mishra (1981: 105).
59 Blake and Ormerod (eds) (1980).
60 'Introduction', ibid., p. 5.
61 ibid., p. 4.
62 ibid., p. 5.
63 Bill Jordan, 'Labour's latest Utopia', *New Society* (23 September 1982: 497).
64 Thurow (1981).
65 ibid., p. 11.
66 ibid., p. 7.
67 ibid.
68 ibid., p. 191.
69 ibid., p. 77.
70 ibid.
71 ibid., p. 84.
72 ibid., p. 85.
73 ibid., ch. 7.
74 ibid., pp. 201-2, 210-11.

75 ibid., pp. 212-13.
76 Room (1979); Furniss and Tilton (1979).
77 Room (1979: 251-2).
78 ibid., pp. 18-23, ch. 7.
79 ibid., p. 20.
80 ibid., p. 23.
81 ibid., p. 259.
82 ibid., p. 258.
83 ibid., p. 259.
84 ibid., ch. 7.
85 ibid., p. 258.
86 Furniss and Tilton (1979: 41).
87 ibid., p. 42.
88 See chs 3 and 4.
89 ibid., p. 41.
90 ibid., p. 58.
91 ibid., p. 80.
92 ibid., pp. 20, 25, 42, 87.
93 ibid., pp. 142, 119.

Chapter 6

1 The so-called Alternative Economic Strategy (AES) is the Labour Left's answer to the current crisis – a socialist alternative to monetarism and social democracy. It includes extensive government control of trade, finance, investment, etc. in order to reflate the British economy and reconstruct British industry. See e.g. CSE (1980); Cripps (1981).

Bibliography

Abel-Smith, Brian and Townsend, Peter (1965), *The Poor and the Poorest* (Bell, London).

Althusser, Louis (1971), *Lenin and Philosophy and other Essays* (New Left Books, London).

Althusser, Louis and Balibar, Etienne (1970), *Reading Capital* (New Left Books, London).

Anderson, James E. (1979), *Public Policy-Making* (Holt, Rinehart & Winston, New York).

Armitage, Andrew (1975), *Social Welfare in Canada* (McClelland & Stewart, Toronto).

Baran, Paul A. and Sweezy, Paul M. (1968), *Monopoly Capital* (Penguin, Harmondsworth).

Baumol, William J. (ed.) (1980), *Public and Private Enterprise in a Mixed Economy* (St Martin's Press, New York).

Bell, Daniel (1976), *The Coming of Post-Industrial Society* (Penguin, Harmondsworth).

Bell, Daniel (1979), *The Cultural Contradictions of Capitalism* (Heinemann, London).

Bennett, J.T. and DiLorenzo, T.J. (1982), 'Off Budget Activities of Local Government. The Bane of the Tax Revolt', *Public Choice* 39 (3).

Beveridge, W.H. (1942), *Social Insurance and Allied Services*, Cmd 6404 (HMSO, London).

Blackburn, Robin (1967), 'Inequality and Exploitation', *New Left Review*, 42.

Blackburn, Robin (ed.) (1972), *Ideology in Social Science* (Fontana, London).

Blake, David and Ormerod, Paul (eds) (1980), *The Economics of Prosperity: Social Priorities in the Eighties* (Grant & McIntyre, 1980).

Bottomore, Tom (ed.) (1975), *Crisis and Contention in Sociology* (Sage, London/Beverly Hills).

Brittan, Samuel (1977), *The Economic Consequences of Democracy* (Temple Smith, London).

Bruce, Maurice (1965), *The Coming of the Welfare State* (Batsford, London).

Buchanan, James M. and Wagner, Richard E. (1977), *Democracy in Deficit* (Academic Press, New York).

Burchell, Robert W. and Sternlieb, George (eds) (1978), *Planning Theory in the 1980s: A Search for Future Directions* (Rutgers University, New Brunswick, NJ).

Castles, Francis G. (1978), *The Social Democratic Image of Society* (Routledge, London).

Centre for Policy Studies (1975), *Why Britain Needs a Social Market Economy* (Centre for Policy Studies, London).

CSE (Conference of Socialist Economists) (1980), *The Alternative Economic Strategy: A Response by the Labour Movement to the Economic Crisis* (CSE Books, London).

Conservative Political Centre (1958), *The Future of the Welfare State* (London).

Corrigan, Paul (1979), 'Popular Consciousness and Social Democracy', *Marxism Today*, 23 (12).

Cripps, Francis (1981), 'The British Crisis – Can the Left Win?', *New Left Review*, 128.

Critical Social Policy (1982), 2 (1).

Crosland, C. A. R. (1964), *The Future of Socialism* (Cape, London) (1st edn 1956).

Crozier, Michel *et al.* (1975), *The Crisis of Democracy: Report on the Governability of Democracies to the Trilateral Commission* (New York University Press, New York).

Davis, Mike (1981) 'The New Right's Road to Power', *New Left Review*, 128.

Dahrendorf, Ralf (1959), *Class and Class Conflict in Industrial Society* (Routledge, London).

Danziger, James N. (1980), 'California's Proposition 13 And The Fiscal Limitations Movement In The United States', *Political Studies*, 28 (4).

Donnison, David, 'Social Policy since Titmuss', *Journal of Social Policy*, 8 (2).

Dorfman, Gerald A. (1979), *Government Versus Trade Unionism in British Politics Since 1968* (Macmillan, London).

Douglas, James (1976), 'Review Article: The Overloaded Crown', *British Journal of Political Science*, 6 (4).

Douglas, James (1981), 'Reagan's Victory', *Political Quarterly*, 52 (2).

Downs, Anthony (1957), *An Economic Theory of Democracy* (Harper & Row, New York).

Duignan, Peter and Rabushka, Albin (eds) (1980), *The United States in the 1980s* (Hoover Institution: Stanford University, Cal.).

Durkheim, Emile (1964), *The Division of Labor in Society* (Free Press, New York).

Field, Frank (1981), *Inequality in Britain* (Fontana, London).

Filo della Torre, Paolo *et al.* (1979), *Eurocommunism: Myth or Reality?* (Penguin, Harmondsworth).

Frank, André Gunder (1970), *Latin America: Underdevelopment or Revolution* (Monthly Review Press, paperback edn, New York).

Frank, André Gunder (1980), *Crisis: In The World Economy* (Heinemann, London).

Friedman, Milton (1962), *Capitalism and Freedom* (University of Chicago Press, Chicago/London).

Friedman, Milton (1977), *From Galbraith to Economic Freedom* (Institute of Economic Affairs, London).

Friedman, Milton and Friedman, Rose (1980), *Free to Choose* (Penguin, Harmondsworth).

Furniss, Norman and Tilton, Timothy (1979), *The Case For The Welfare State* (Indiana University Press, paperback edn, Bloomington/London).

Galbraith, J.K. (1958), *The Affluent Society* (Houghton Mifflin, Boston).

Gamble, Andrew and Walton, Paul (1976), *Capitalism in Crisis* (Macmillan, London).

Gans, Herbert J. (1972), 'The Positive Functions of Poverty', *American Journal of Sociology*, 78 (2).

George, Vic and Manning, Nick (1980), *Socialism, Social Welfare and the Soviet Union* (Routledge, London).

George, Vic and Wilding, Paul (1976), *Ideology and Social Welfare* (Routledge, London).

Giddens, Anthony (1973), *The Class Structure of Advanced Societies* (Hutchinson, London).

Gilder, George (1982), *Wealth and Poverty* (Bantam Books, New York).

Ginsburg, Norman (1979), *Class, Capital and Social Policy* (Macmillan, London).

Goldthorpe, J. H. (1964), 'Social Stratification in Industrial Society', in *The Development of Industrial Societies*, Sociological Review Monograph no. 8 (University of Keele, Keele).

Gosden, P. H. J. H. (1973), *Self-Help: Voluntary Associations in Nineteenth-century Britain* (Batsford, London).

Gough, Ian (1975), 'State Expenditure in Advanced Capitalism', *New Left Review*, 92.

Gough, Ian (1979), *The Political Economy of the Welfare State* (Macmillan, London).

Gouldner, Alvin W. (1971), *The Coming Crisis of Western Sociology* (Heinemann, London).

Grønbjerg, Kirsten A. (1977), *Mass Society and the Extension of Welfare 1960-1970* (University of Chicago Press, Chicago).

Grønbjerg, Kirsten *et al.* (1978), *Poverty and Social Change* (University of Chicago Press, Chicago).

Guest, Dennis (1980), *The Emergence of Social Security in Canada* (University of British Columbia Press, Vancouver).

Habermas, Jürgen (1972), *Knowledge and Human Interests* (Heinemann, London).

Habermas, Jürgen (1976), *Legitimation Crisis* (Heinemann, London).

Habermas, Jürgen (1979), 'Conservatism and Capitalist Crisis', *New Left Review*, 115.

Hall, Stuart (1979), 'The Great Moving Right Show', *Marxism Today*, 23 (1).

Harrington, Michael (1962), *The Other America* (Macmillan, New York).

Hayek, F. A. (1944), *The Road to Serfdom* (Routledge, London).

Hayek, F. A. (1973), *Economics Freedom and Representative Government* (Institute of Economic Affairs, London).

Hayek, F. A. (1976), *Law, Legislation and Liberty Vol. 2: The Mirage of Social Justice* (Routledge, London).

Hayek, F. A. (1978), *New Studies in Philosophy, Politics, Economics and the History of Ideas* (University of Chicago Press, Chicago).

Hirsch, Fred (1978), *Social Limits to Growth* (Routledge, London).

Hirsch, Fred and Goldthorpe, John H. (eds) (1978), *The Political Economy of Inflation* (Harvard University Press, Cambridge, Mass.).

Holloway, John and Picciotto, Sol (eds) (1978), *State and Capital* (Arnold, London).

Hoos, Ida R. (1972), *Systems Analysis in Public Policy: A Critique* (University of California Press, Berkeley/Los Angeles).

Horowitz, I. L. (ed.) (1979), *Constructing Policy* (Praeger, New York).

Janowitz, Morris (1976), *Social Control of the Welfare State* (University of Chicago Press, Chicago).

Jessop, Bob (1977), 'Recent Theories of the Capitalist State', *Cambridge Journal of Economics*, 1 (4).

Johnson, Terence J. (1972), *Professions and Power* (Macmillan, London).

Jones, H. G. (1976), *Planning and Productivity in Sweden* (Croom Helm, London).

Jones, Phil (1980), 'The Thatcher Experiment', *Politics and Power 2* (Routledge, London).

Kaldor, Mary (1979), *the Disintegrating West* (Penguin, Harmondsworth).

Kerr, Clark *et al.* (1973), *Industrialism and Industrial Man* (Penguin, Harmondsworth).

King, Anthony (1973), 'Ideas, Institutions and the Policies of Governments; a Comparative Analysis', *British Journal of Political Science*, 3 (3).

King, Anthony (1975), 'Overload: Problems of Governing In The 1970s', *Political Studies*, 23 (2, 3).

Kolko, Gabriel (1962), *Wealth and Power in America* (Praeger, New York).

Kristol, Irving (1978), *Two Cheers for Capitalism* (Basic Books, New York).

Kumar, Krishan (1978), *Prophecy and Progress* (Penguin, Harmondsworth).

196

Lane, David (1976), *The Socialist Industrial State* (Allen & Unwin, London).

LeGrand, Julian (1982), *The Strategy of Equality* (Allen & Unwin, London).

Leiby, James (1978), *A History of Social Welfare and Social Work in the United States* (Columbia University Press, New York).

Lewis, Stephen and Harrison, Anthony (1981), 'Public Spending: A Failure of Control?', *Public Money*, 1 (1).

Lipset, S. M. (1969), *Political Man* (Heinemann, London).

Loew, Raimund, 'The Politics of the Austrian "Miracle"', *New Left Review*, 123.

Mandel, Ernest (1968), *Marxist Economic Theory* (Merlin Press, London).

Mao Tse Tung (1967), *On Contradiction* (Foreign Languages Press, Peking).

Marcuse, Herbert (1968), *One Dimensional Man* (Sphere Books, London).

Marris, Peter and Rein, Martin (1974), *Dilemmas of Social Reform* (Penguin, Harmondsworth).

Marshall, T. H. (1963), *Sociology at the Crossroads* (Heinemann, London).

Marshall, T. H. (1965), *Social Policy* (Hutchinson, London).

Marshall, T. H. (1981), *The Right to Welfare and Other Essays* (Heinemann, London).

Matthews, R. C. O. *et al.* (1982), *British Economic Growth 1854-1973* (Stanford University Press, Cal.).

McIntosh, Mary (1981), 'Feminism and Social Policy', *Critical Social Policy*, 1 (1).

Meacher, Michael (1982), *Socialism with a Human Face* (Allen & Unwin, London).

Meissner, Hanna H. (ed.) (1966), *Poverty In The Affluent Society* (Harper & Row, New York).

Miliband, Ralph (1973), *The State in Capitalist Society* (Quartet Books, London) (1st edn 1969).

Mishra, Ramesh (1973), 'Welfare and Industrial Man', *Sociological Review*, NS 21 (4).

Mishra, Ramesh (1976), 'Convergence Theory and Social Change: The Development of Welfare in Britain and the

Soviet Union', *Comparative Studies in Society and History*, 18 (1).

Mishra, Ramesh (1981), *Society and Social Policy* (Macmillan, London).

Mishra, Ramesh (1982), 'System Integration, Social Action and Change', *Sociological Review*, NS 30(1).

Moynihan, Daniel Patrick (1965), 'The Professionalization of Reform', *The Public Interest*, 1.

Moynihan, Daniel P. (1973), *Coping* (Random House, New York).

Navarro, Vincente (1982), 'The Crisis of the International Capitalist Order and its Implications for the Welfare State', *Critical Social Policy*, 2(1).

Niskanen, William A. Jr (1971), *Bureaucracy and Representative Government* (Aldine, Chicago).

O'Connor, James (1973), *The Fiscal Crisis of the State* (St Martin's Press, New York).

O'Connor, James (1981), 'The Fiscal Crisis of the State Revisited', *Kapitalistate*, 9.

OECD (1976), *Public Expenditure on Income Maintenance Programmes* (Paris).

OECD (1977), *Public Expenditure on Health* (Paris).

OECD (1978), *Public Expenditure Trends* (Paris).

OECD (1980), 'Incomes Policy in Theory and Practice', *Economic Outlook: Occasional Studies*, July 1980 (Paris).

OECD (1981), *The Welfare State in Crisis* (Paris).

OECD (1981a), *Integrated Social Policy: A Review of the Austrian Experience* (Paris).

OECD (1981b), *Economic Surveys: Austria* (Paris).

OECD (1981c), *Economic Surveys: Sweden* (Paris).

OECD (1982), *Economic Surveys 1981-1982: Austria* (Paris).

OECD (1982a), *Economic Surveys 1981-1982: Sweden* (Paris).

Parkin, Frank (1971), *Class Inequality and Political Order* (Paladin, London).

Parkin, Frank (1972), 'System Contradiction and Political Transformation', *European Journal of Sociology*, 13(1).

Parsons, Talcott (1951), *The Social System* (Routledge, London).

Parsons, Talcott (1971), *The System of Modern Societies* (Prentice-Hall, Englewood Cliffs, NJ).

Peretz, Paul (1982), 'There Was No Tax Revolt!', *Politics and Society*, 11(2).

Phillips, Kevin P. (1982), *Post-Conservative America* (Random House, New York).

Pinker, Robert (1971), *Social Theory and Social Policy* (Heinemann, London).

Pinker, Robert (1979), *The Idea of Welfare* (Heinemann, London).

Politics and Power, 2 (1980) (Routledge, London).

Popper, K. R. (1957), *The Open Society And Its Enemies* vol. II (Routledge, London).

Popper, Karl R. (1961), *The Poverty of Historicism* (Routledge, London).

Poulantzas, Nicos (1973), *Political Power and Social Classes* (New Left Books, London) (1st edn 1968).

Poulantzas, Nicos (1975), *Classes in Contemporary Capitalism* (New Left Books, London).

Rawls, John (1971), *A Theory of Justice* (Harvard University Press, Cambridge, Mass.).

Rayner, Geof (1982), 'The Reagonomics of Welfare', *Critical Social Policy*, 2 (1).

Reisman, D. A. (1977), *Richard Titmuss* (Heinemann, London).

Rex, John (1974), *Sociology and the Demystification of the Modern World* (Routledge, London).

Rex, John (ed.) (1974a), *Approaches To Sociology* (Routledge, London).

Richardson, Paul (1975), *Britain, Europe and the Modern World 1918-1974* (Heinemann, 1975).

Rimlinger, Gaston V. (1971), *Welfare Policy and Industrialization in Europe, America and Russia* (John Wiley, New York).

Robson, William A. (1976), *Welfare State and Welfare Society* (Allen & Unwin, London).

Roby, Pamela (ed.) (1974), *The Poverty Establishment* (Prentice-Hall, Englewood Cliffs, NJ).

Room, Graham (1979), *The Sociology of Welfare* (Blackwell, Oxford).

Rose, Hilary and Rose, Steven (1982), 'Moving Right Out of Welfare and the Way Back', *Critical Social Policy*, 2(1).

Rustin, Michael (1980), 'The New Left and the Crisis', *New Left Review*, 121.

Saville, John (1957-8), 'The Welfare State: An Historical Approach', *New Reasoner*, 3.

Schmitter, Phillipe C. and Lehmbruch, Gerhard (eds) (1979), *Trends Toward Corporatist Intermediation* (Sage, London/ Beverly Hills).

Schottland, Charles I. (ed.) (1967), *The Welfare State* (Harper & Row, New York).

Schonfield, Andrew (1969), *Modern Capitalism* (Oxford University Press, New York).

Silverman, David (1970) *The Theory of Organisations* (Heinemann, London).

Skidelsky, Robert (ed.) (1977), *The End Of The Keynesian Era* (Macmillan, London).

Smith, Anthony D. (1973), *The Concept of Social Change* (Routledge, London).

Smith, Trevor (1979), *The Politics of the Corporate Economy* (Martin Robertson, Oxford).

Stein, M. *et al.* (1982), 'Personal Social Services under the Conservatives', *Critical Social Policy*, 1(3).

Steinfels, Peter (1979), *The Neoconservatives* (Simon & Schuster, New York).

Stoffaës, Christian (ed.) (1982), *The Political Economy of the United States* (North Holland, New York).

Tawney, R. H. (1966), *The Radical Tradition* (Penguin, Harmondsworth).

Taylor-Gooby, Peter and Dale, Jennifer (1981), *Social Theory and Social Welfare* (Arnold, London).

Thurow, Lester C. (1981), *The Zero-Sum Society* (Penguin, New York).

Titmuss, Richard M. (1962), *Income Distribution and Social Change* (Allen & Unwin, London).

Titmuss, Richard M. (1963), *Essays on 'The Welfare State'* (Allen & Unwin, London).

Titmuss, Richard M. (1968), *Commitment to Welfare* (Allen & Unwin, London).

Titmuss, Richard M. (1974), *Social Policy* (Allen & Unwin, London).

Townsend, Peter (1962), 'The Meaning of Poverty', *British Journal of Sociology*, 13(3).

Bibliography

Townsend, Peter (1979), *Poverty in the United Kingdom* (Allen Lane, London).

Townsend, Peter (1980), 'Politics and Social Policy: An Interview', *Politics and Power*, 2 (Routledge, London).

Townsend, Peter and Bosanquet, Nicholas (eds) (1972), *Labour and Inequality* (Fabian Society, London).

Union for Radical Political Economics (1981), *Crisis in the Public Sector* (Monthly Review Press, New York).

Walker, Alan (1980), 'A Right Turn for the British Welfare State?', *Social Policy*, 10(5).

Weaver, Findley (1950), 'Taxation and Redistribution in the United Kingdom', *Review of Economics and Statistics*, 32(3).

Webb, A.L. and Sieve, J.E.B. (1971), *Income Redistribution and the Welfare State* (Bell, London).

Weber, Max (1930) *Protestant Ethic and the Spirit of Capitalism* (Allen & Unwin, London).

Weed, Frank J. (1979), 'Industrialization and Welfare System', *International Journal of Comparative Sociology*, 20 (3-4).

Weinberg, Ian (1969), 'The Problem of the Convergence of Industrial Societies', *Comparative Studies in Society and History* 11(1).

Weinberger, Paul E. (ed.) (1974), *Perspectives On Social Welfare* (Macmillan, New York).

Westergaard, John and Resler, Henrietta (1976), *Class in a Capitalist Society* (Penguin, Harmondsworth).

Wildavsky, Aaron (1980), *The Art and Craft of Policy Analysis* (Macmillan, London).

Wilding, Paul (1976), 'Richard Titmuss and Social Welfare', *Social and Economic Administration*, 10(3).

Wilensky, Harold L. and Lebeaux, Charles N. (1965), *Industrial Society and Social Welfare* (Free Press, New York).

Wilensky, Harold L. (1975), *The Welfare State and Equality* (University of California Press, Berkeley/Los Angeles).

Wilensky, Harold L. (1976), *The 'New Corporatism', Centralization, and the Welfare State* (Sage, London/Beverly Hills).

Willer, David and Willer, Judith (1973), *Systematic Empiricism* (Prentice-Hall, Englewood Cliffs, NJ).

Williamson, John B. and Flemming, Jeane J. (1977), 'Convergence Theory and the Social Welfare Sector', *International Journal of Comparative Sociology*, 18 (3-4).

201

Wilson, Elizabeth (1980), 'The Political Economy of Welfare', *New Left Review*, 122.

Winch, Donald (1972), *Economics and Policy* (Fontana, London).

Wolfe, Alan (1981), 'Sociology, Liberalism, and the Radical Right', *New Left Review*, 128.

Index of Names

Index of Subjects